BLUEPRINTS

Maths Teacher's Resource Book Key Stage 1

Wendy and David Clemson

Stanley Thornes (Publishers) Ltd

Text © Wendy and David Clemson 1992
Original line illustrations © Stanley Thornes (Publishers) Ltd 1992
Illustrations by Tim Smith

Material from *Mathematics in the National Curriculum, 1991* is reproduced with the permission of the Controller of Her Majesty's Stationery Office.

First published in 1992 by
Stanley Thornes (Publishers) Ltd
Old Station Drive
Leckhampton
CHELTENHAM GL53 0DN
England

A catalogue record for this book is available from the British Library.

ISBN 0-7487-0577-5

Typeset by Tech-Set, Gateshead, Tyne & Wear.
Printed at The Bath Press, Avon.

Contents

Introduction

In order to be able to extract meaning from the world around us it is essential that we become numerate, just as we need to be literate and able to deploy language in a variety of ways. Both natural and designed environments are explicable in some respects only through mathematics. To be deprived of the skills necessary to understand the constants and variables in the world is to be both intellectually and practically disadvantaged. It is therefore vitally important that all children are exposed to the challenge, beauty, relevance and breadth of mathematics. But to communicate all this demands enlivening teaching and learning.

Mathematicians in the making need enthusiastic mathematicians as teachers. If you yourself find maths the most irksome part of the curriculum, please give it another go! Mathematics is essentially about pattern. Human beings search for patterns in experience in order to understand the world. Mathematics unites language and science. Mathematics is not a 'way of thinking' independent of language, but a realisation that mathematics is pattern enriches thinking and understanding. Mathematics also engages us in the measurement of shapes, spaces and comparisons.

To measure is to try to obtain some information about the environment. We attempt to describe the passing of time through the use of regular intervals, and we produce scale maps of road systems. We offer for sale products which can be compared in terms of their size and quantity, and national economies are geared to the quantity of raw materials and the cost of turning these materials into artifacts. Measurement is at the heart of civilisation.

If every child leaves your class able to construct and read a block graph, for example, they are *all* on the way to becoming competent mathematicians, and that is something you can take credit for and be proud of. Whatever the future of the nation, simply by looking at ways of interpreting data you will have influenced some of the lives of the children with whom you have worked. Never underestimate the capabilities of young children, the power of mathematics or the influence of the teacher!

WHAT IS BLUEPRINTS MATHS?

Blueprints Maths is a practical, teacher's resource specifically written to fulfil the requirements of the National Curriculum in maths for primary schools. It is intended for all teachers, particularly those who are not maths specialists, and provides comprehensive coverage in an easy-to-follow format. *Blueprints Maths* is a rich resource of practical ideas to use alongside other materials within your scheme of work. It gives children meaningful, relevant things to do. *Blueprints Maths Key Stage 1* provides activities for 5–7 year olds; *Blueprints Maths Key Stage 2* provides activities for 7–11 year olds. For each key stage there is a *Teacher's Resource Book* and a book of *Pupils' Copymasters*.

The *Teacher's Resource Book* and the accompanying *Pupils' Copymasters* follow closely the structure of the *Mathematics in the National Curriculum (1991)*. The *Teacher's Resource Book* is arranged in sections, each corresponding to work in a National Curriculum Attainment Target. The *Pupils' Copymasters* match the activities in each Attainment Target.

The *Blueprints Maths Key Stage 1 Teacher's Resource Book* provides dozens of lively activities through Key Stage 1. The book is arranged in four main sections, each relating to work expected of children through this Key Stage, covering Attainment Targets 2, 3, 4 and 5 at Levels 1–3. A discussion about how to cover AT1 appears at the front of the book. At the start of each Attainment Target and at each Level there is an extract from the Statutory Orders, comprising the AT title, the appropriate Programme of Study, the Statements of Attainment and Non-Statutory Guidance.

The *Teacher's Resource Book* will prove an invaluable resource, even without the use of the pupils' copymasters. You can, in developing your own schemes of work, choose activities to fit those aspects on which you are focusing. There is a record sheet at the back of the book, on which you can identify activities the children have tried, and also note work done contributing to AT 1.

The *Pupils' Copymasters* book provides 115 photocopiable worksheets. C1–C103 are linked specifically to many of the activities in the *Teacher's Resource Book*. R1–R11 are resource copymasters and can be used again and again across all sections of the book. When completed, the worksheets can be added to the children's workfiles or used as exemplar material in pupil profiles. They may also be seen as a resource for teacher assessment. There is a tick list at the back of the book, on which you can note the photocopy sheets the children have made use of.

Blueprints Maths Key Stage 1 provides coverage of Attainment Targets 2–5 for Levels 1–3. It is expected that most children should master Level 2 but Level 3 work is provided for those children who require work beyond Level 2.

The *Pupils' Copymasters* are provided as support for

busy teachers and to provide a framework for recording the children's achievement.

Attainment Target 1

Attainment Target 1, Using and applying mathematics, has been treated differently from the other ATs. At the beginning of the book you will find a brief summary of how you can incorporate work on AT 1 into the activities the children do.

Record keeping

There are photocopiable record sheets at the back of the *Teacher's Resource Book* and the *Pupils' Copymasters* book. Photocopy one *Teacher's Resource Book* record sheet per child and the Levels of the appropriate ATs the child has worked at. Photocopy one *Pupils' Copymaster* record sheet per child and tick the photocopy sheets each child has worked on.

How to use this book

This book has been tied to National Curriculum Attainment Targets so that you can access the activities easily. Within each of the sections:

- Number
- Algebra
- Shape and space
- Handling data

the activities have been arranged by Level, with Level 1 activities first, and so on.

At the beginning is a discussion of how to achieve coverage of Attainment Target 1, which demands a different treatment in that it 'threads through' the other Attainment Targets.

Our intention is not that the activities should be worked through in linear fashion. We hope that you will dip into the book and use the activities where they are appropriate. We would favour an approach where, for a period of time, which may be a day or weeks, you involve all the children in activities in, for example,

algebra (AT 3), at whatever Levels they are working. The activities will also support thematic work where a number of curriculum areas are involved at the same time. For example, the shape and space activities (AT 4) would enhance, and themselves be enhanced by, work in art, PE and music.

At the end of the book you will find a record sheet, which will enable you to register a child's contact with work on each Attainment Target at a Level.

If you also have the *Pupils' Copymasters* use them to support learning and help with consolidation, assessment and evaluation where appropriate. You will find the copymasters referred to in this book with the symbol:

Copymasters 1–103 are tied to activities in Number, Algebra, Shape and space, and Handling data. **Copymasters R1–R11** can be used again and again as general resources across all the sections of the book.

RESOURCING YOUR MATHEMATICS

Most of the resources you and the children need for mathematics are commonly and readily available. In the activities in each section we assume you have such things as pots and containers, collections of objects, and so on; these general resources are listed below. At the beginning of each section, you will find suggestions for additions to the general resources that will help in working in that particular section.

In addition to the children themselves, you will need a resource bank in the classroom, easily accessible to you and preferably also to the children. Pencils, crayons, books, rulers and the like are in most classrooms. Some of these can be set aside as maths resources, for the time that they are needed. Some commercially produced counting aids, like Unifix®, Colour Factor®, Cuisenaire®, Multilink® and Centicubes® are commonly available in most schools and are extremely useful. Here are some suggestions for other possible resources:

- Beads, conkers and other nuts, shells, marbles, sticks, timber offcuts, wooden blocks, cotton reels, pressed and mounted leaves, seeds, feathers, egg cups, spoons, soft toys, model farm animals, dolls' house furniture and dolls, model cars, socks, balls of wool, spent matches, elastic bands, pebbles and pieces of string, heavy rope, skipping rope

- Containers, cartons and boxes of all kinds, including jugs, beakers, jars and plastic bottles, tins, yogurt pots, margarine tubs, matchboxes, food boxes, egg boxes and boxes big enough for children to get into
- Marbles, beads, dice and spinners
- Building bricks, Duplo®, Lego®, Plasticine®, clay, play dough (see opposite) and 'play food' or other items made with this, drinking straws and Artstraws®
- Pictures from magazines and catalogues, old greeting cards and postcards
- Number lines, play money, metre sticks, cardboard clock face; rubber stamps with pictures, numbers, coins or shapes on them; number games, calculators
- Fabrics, metal objects and samples of natural materials
- A wide variety of art materials, including a range of varieties of paper, cardboard, gummed shapes, scissors, sticky tape, chalks, brushes, paints and inks.

In addition to these general resources we have found some further items of particular value. These are:

- Blank dice, which can be bought through educational suppliers, and can be written on with felt-tip pen, or have stick-on numerals attached
- Many-sided dice, obtainable from shops selling elaborate board games

● Play dough, which can be made as follows: Stir together 2 cups unsifted flour, 1 cup salt, 1 cup (approximately) water and 2 tablespoons cooking oil. This recipe comes from *The Playgroup Book* by Marie Winn and Mary Ann Porcher. Experiment with the proportions until the consistency is such that it holds its shape. Play dough can be hardened by placing models in a low-temperature oven to dry out. It then takes powder paint well and can be varnished. If you want a batch of, for example, badges or fruits of one colour, food colouring can be added with the water when the dough is made up.

BOOKS ▶

Books are also necessary. We enclose a starter list of children's books here, which we have drawn up with the help of *Books for Infant Mathematics*, produced by the Association of Teachers of Mathematics.

Story books

Ahlberg, A. and J., *Burglar Bill*, Heinemann/Mammoth
Anno, M., *Anno's Flea Market*, Bodley Head
Berenstein, S. and J., *Inside, Outside, Upside Down*, Collins
Blake, Q., *Mister Magnolia*, J Cape
Briggs, R., *Jim and the Beanstalk*, Picture Puffin
Burningham, J., *The Shopping Basket*, J Cape
Carle, E., *The Very Hungry Caterpillar*, Puffin
Hedderwick, M., *Katie Morag and the Two Grandmothers*, Armada
Hughes, S., *Alfie Gets in First*, Armada
Hutchins, P., *Don't Forget the Bacon*, Picture Puffin
Hutchins, P., *Rosie's Walk*, Bodley Head/Puffin
Kerr, J., *Mog in the Dark*, Armada
Lord, J. V., *The Giant Jam Sandwich*, Pan Books
Nicoll, H. and Pienkowski, J., *Meg and Mog*, Picture Puffin
Nicoll, H. and Pienkowski, J., *Owl at School*, Picture Puffin
Sutton, E., *My Cat Likes to Hide in Boxes*, Picture Puffin

Tolstoy, A. and Oxenbury, H., *The Great Big Enormous Turnip*, Armada
Vipont, E. and Briggs, R., *The Elephant and the Bad Baby*, Picture Puffin

Counting books

Adams, P., *There were Ten in the Bed*, Childs Play
Bradman, T., *The Bad Babies Counting Book*, Piccadilly/Beaver
Gretz, S., *Teddy Bears 1 to 10*, Collins
Peppe, R., *Circus Numbers*, Viking Kestrel

Books for teachers

Finally, we should like to recommend these books for teachers:

Deboys, M. and Pitt, E. (1980) *Lines of Development in Primary Mathematics* (2nd ed.), Blackstaff Press
Hughes, M. (1986) *Children and Number*, Basil Blackwell
Merttens, R. (1987) *Teaching Primary Maths*, Edward Arnold
Williams, E. and Shuard, H. (1982) *Primary Mathematics Today* (3rd ed.), Longman

Also the Association of Teachers of Mathematics and the Mathematical Association produce a wide range of booklets and other resources.

ATTAINMENT TARGET 1
Using and applying mathematics

Attainment Target 1: Using and applying mathematics

Pupils should choose and make use of knowledge, skills and understanding outlined in the programmes of study in practical tasks, in real-life problems and to investigate within mathematics itself. Pupils would be expected to use with confidence the appropriate mathematical content specified in the programmes of study relating to the other attainment targets.

Attainment Target 1 'threads through' Attainment Targets 2–5. We are confident that if the children with whom you are working have experience of a wide variety of the activities in this book, they will embrace the demands of Attainment Target 1. To illustrate this we discuss below, under the relevant statutory orders, the key aspects which should be regularly in evidence while children are engaged in mathematical tasks in your classroom and school.

1

Attainment Target 1: Using and applying mathematics, Level 1

Pupils should choose and make use of knowledge, skills and understanding outlined in the programmes of study in practical tasks, in real-life problems and to investigate within mathematics itself. Pupils would be expected to use with confidence the appropriate mathematical content specified in the programmes of study relating to the other attainment targets.

Programme of study	Statements of attainment	Examples
Pupils should engage in activities which involve:	Pupils should be able to:	Pupils could:
• using materials for a practical task.	a) Use mathematics as an integral part of practical classroom tasks.	*Use measuring in cooking.* *Build symmetrical 3-D models.*
• talking about their work and asking questions.	b) Talk about their own work and respond to questions.	*Describe how to play a counting game.* *Talk about the sizes of the different types of flower they have collected.* *Use signs to discuss which toy car rolled the furthest and whether it was the biggest one.*
• making predictions based on experience.	c) Make predictions based on experience.	*Use a balance to compare objects; predict which of the two objects will be the heavier.* *Gain experience of the school day; predict when the class with be in the hall for music and dance.*

At the start, and all through as far as possible, the children should have a variety of concrete objects to handle in the course of their maths. Look at the suggested resource bank in 'Resourcing your mathematics' for ideas.

Children should be able to talk about their work continuously. Let them talk to you and to each other while they do it and when they have done it. Encourage 'reporting back' at the end of the session or day. It is one thing to understand what you have done – it is quite another to explain it to others so that they understand too!

Once the children had a few 'goes' at an activity, you can encourage them to begin to say what may happen if they do a similar activity again, or if the circumstances change a little. The children will not only begin to formulate 'hypotheses' that they can test, but they will also start to make connections and links between things they know.

Attainment Target 1: Using and applying mathematics, Level 2

Pupils should choose and make use of knowledge, skills and understanding outlined in the programmes of study in practical tasks, in real-life problems and to investigate within mathematics itself. Pupils would be expected to use with confidence the appropriate mathematical content specified in the programmes of study relating to the other attainment targets.

Programme of study	Statements of attainment	Examples
Pupils should engage in activities which involve:	Pupils should be able to:	Pupils could:
• selecting the materials and the mathematics to use for a practical task.	a) Select the materials and the mathematics to use for a practical task.	*Choose to use buckets and bathroom scales to find out which of four classes collected the most conkers.* *Sort and classify a collection of coloured plane shapes using own criteria.* *Understand that if one child has five pencils and another three pencils, the total number is found by addition.*
• describing work and checking results.	b) Talk about work or ask questions using appropriate mathematical language.	*Talk about how they decided to collect information about which food birds prefer and ways to make the information clear.* *Describe how a classification of shapes was made.* *Describe how they made a hat that fitted.*
• asking and responding to questions, e.g. 'What would happen if ...?', 'Why ...?'	c) Respond appropriately to the question: 'What would happen if ...?'	*Explain that the same amount of water would come to a higher level in a jam jar than in a bowl because the jar is thinner.* *Predict that the next brick out of the bag is likely to be red as there are more of them.* *Discuss a block graph showing the ways children in the class came to school that morning; respond to the question: 'How will the graph change if there are no buses running tomorrow?'*

There is much talk in the National Curriculum of the 'independent learner'. At Level 2 the independent mathematician begins to emerge. If the children are given choices and chances to resource their own work, they will soon be able to do so with confidence. All that is necessary for a task must be readily accessible, and children and teacher must agree on the procedures for putting away the resources afterwards.

At this Level the children should not only be given opportunities to talk about their work while they are doing it and after they have completed it, but with your help they should begin to write down the outcomes.

With increased breadth of experience of practical mathematical activity the children will begin to speculate about extending the activities they are trying. When they say, for example, 'I wonder what would happen if I put . . . another ball of Plasticine® on the balance?' or '. . . another 4 in this set?' or '. . . another +2 into the calculator?', they are taking ownership of and going beyond the activity. They can proceed to solve the new problem with your guidance and say whether what happened matched what they expected and why it happened.

3

Attainment Target 1: Using and applying mathematics, Level 3

Pupils should choose and make use of knowledge, skills and understanding outlined in the programmes of study in practical tasks, in real-life problems and to investigate within mathematics itself. Pupils would be expected to use with confidence the appropriate mathematical content specified in the programmes of study relating to the other attainment targets.

Programme of study	Statements of attainment	Examples
Pupils should engage in activities which involve:	Pupils should be able to:	Pupils could:
• selecting the materials and the mathematics to use for a task using alternative approaches to overcome difficulties.	a) Find ways of overcoming difficulties when solving problems.	*Work out that ten 9s are 90 and add three 9s to this when multiplying 13 by 9 to give the number of tiles in the classroom. When measuring orange juice, and the jug looks like overflowing, think of filling the jug, pouring into a bowl, measuring the rest and adding the two results together. Design and make a weather vane which involves symmetry; test and modify.*
• explaining work and recording findings systematically.	b) Use or interpret appropriate mathematical aspects of everyday language in a precise way.	*Explain methods of calculation using correct terminology. Describe their model train using names for 3-D and 2-D shapes. Read the instructions for a dice game involving words like 'multiply', 'add', and 'total', and explain to others in a group what to do. Describe the weather vane and its function using appropriate terms.*
• investigating and testing predictions, and general statements.	c) Present results in a clear and organised way.	*Keep a record of the weather over a period of time; display the results in an appropriate chart. Record their results clearly without omissions when working out which numbers are in both the 3- and 4-times-tables.*
• checking results, considering whether they are sensible.	d) Investigate general statements by trying out some examples.	*Investigate the possible total amount of money they might have when told someone has exactly three coins. Explore what happens when you add pairs of odd and even numbers.*

You can now help the children to develop their capacity to make mathematical hypotheses and carry through tests of these, by letting them carry out their own investigations using the resources they choose beyond the end of a session, and continuing a line of work until they are ready to take on a new problem.

With the practice in talking about their maths that they have had at Levels 1 and 2, they should be ready and able to begin reporting orally what happens in their activities and writing down outcomes in a way that makes them easy for everyone to understand, using the language of the mathematician where appropriate.

At Level 3 children's practice in estimation will support their learning. Such practice will have helped them to understand that if they know roughly what to expect in terms of an answer they can say whether their answer is likely to be correct. The children should now not only be adept at resourcing their mathematical activities, but also at making judgements about answers, outcomes, results and progress so far, in the light of their own notions of what should happen.

ATTAINMENT TARGET 2
Number

Attainment Target 2: Number

Pupils should understand and use number, including estimation and approximation, interpreting results and checking for reasonableness.

Number is one of the two major building blocks of mathematics, the other being *shape and space*. Without a sense of number and an appreciation of the power of number, children cannot make progress into areas of mathematics such as *algebra* and *data handling*.

In one sense it could be argued that number has been, and continues to be, the major pre-occupation of primary school mathematics for it partly matches the old arithmetic of the 'three R's'. Even a cursory glance into many primary schools would provide ample evidence that children's mathematical experience can be directly linked to the doing of sums.

What the National Curriculum offers, though, is a much broader definition of mathematics than pages of sums, for the requirements in relation to number work are themselves much broader than what has been traditionally offered. In order to grapple with number work in the context of the National Curriculum, children and teachers have to embrace a wide range of activities, many of them not amenable to pencil-and-paper operations. For example, where exploration and appreciation of number patterns may once have been seen by some as recreational mathematics (not proper maths!) it is now seen as an essential part of the ways children can come to understand number. The aim is to enable children to manipulate and use number rather than be its servants. In this section of the book we offer a range of practical activities and, where

appropriate, paper-and-pencil opportunities through which children can start on the road to using numbers for their own purposes – and to do so with a sense of enjoyment and achievement.

Resourcing number

In addition to a selection of the resources we have listed at the beginning of this book, the following will prove useful in carrying through some of the activities in this section:

● A play house with tea-set, dolls, a play table and chairs, and pans and a play cooker, purses, handbags, hats, paper flowers
● Play food, including some made in two halves
● A telephone book, bathroom scales, pretend parcels
● Plastic money and play paper notes
● Containers of different shapes and volumes and measuring jugs
● Balances and scales and standard 'weights'
● Egg timers and interval timers and the raw materials to make sand, water and candle clocks, clocks and stopwatches and play clock faces
● Some pendulum and rocker devices and timers
● Rules and tapes (both metric and imperial) and trundle wheels
● A freezer thermometer and a maximum and minimum thermometer.

Attainment Target 2: Number, Level 1

Pupils should understand and use number, including estimation and approximation, interpreting results and checking for reasonableness.

Programme of study	Statements of attainment	Examples
Pupils should engage in activities which involve:	Pupils should be able to:	Pupils could:
• counting, reading, writing and ordering numbers to at least 10. • learning that the size of a set is given by the last number in the count. • understanding the language associated with number, e.g. 'more', 'fewer', 'the same'. • understanding conservation of number. • making a sensible estimate of a number of objects up to 10.	a) Use number in the context of the classroom and school.	*Count two piles of identical objects (e.g. toy cars, animals), and say which would make the longer line. Estimate the number of apples in a bag. Use sign language to communicate to the school secretary the number of pupils absent from the class that day.*
• using addition and subtraction, with numbers no greater that 10, in the context of real objects.	b) Add and subtract using a small number of objects.	*Given a set of familiar objects, add or remove a stated number.*

BEGINNING COUNTING ▶

Commentary

The emphasis should be on counting things that the children can see, point to, touch and handle. Work with the children in small groups so that they can all touch the items being counted, if they wish.

Encourage the children to count from left to right along a row of items. As far as possible, always present the items for counting like this during the work at Level 1.

The children need plenty of practice in counting real things. Most of the mathematics used in everyday life is based on this; through their own practical experiences, children will come to understand that counting and maths are about real life, and are important and useful.

Much maths is about comparisons, so help the children to compare numbers and find ways of connecting them.

Do not introduce numerals or ask children to record too soon. Recording the result of a count is a separate operation, and not part of the count. Numerals form a new language for children. The children should, for example, have an understanding of what 'two' of many different things look and feel like – and where they might find 'twos' – before they are introduced to the squiggle '2' used as a sign for 'two'.

Activity 1: The children themselves

Get a small group of children to sit close to you, facing you. Ask a child to stand in front of the group, and while you point, let the children count aloud with you. Point to his/her legs, ears, pigtails, buttons, shoes, fingers and any other features that can be counted, like badges or stripes. Restrict your choices to numbers lower than ten. As far as possible, point and count from left to right *from the children's point of view*.

When the children have seen you point and count, and have counted along with you many times, they can each have turns at pointing and counting. Their practice in counting from left to right with you should transfer to their own counting.

When the children are familiar with group counting, ask more children to stand in front of the group to enable counting of 'sorts'. For example, the children can count the number of boys, girls, people with blue eyes, big toes, cardigans, etc.

They can look at and compare numbers of things; for example, you can ask all the children with cardigans to stand in a separate row from those without.

Activity 2: Counting everyday objects

Assemble collections of like objects with ten in each. Conkers and pencils, crayons and rulers, books and

6

blocks are fine, but do make sure your collections include things of varying sizes, materials and colours, and containers with a range of different contents, so that the children understand that all these factors are irrelevant in counting. You could have a variety of different sized cereal packets; a collection of socks, including ones for a baby and an adult's walking or football sock; a set of hats, including a rain hat, felt hat, paper party hat and a doll's hat. Add a dolls' house chair to a row of classroom chairs, a paperhanging brush to your collection of paintbrushes; include full and empty jam-jars in a collection, and several varieties in a collection of nuts.

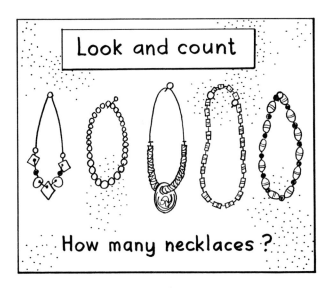

Look and count

How many necklaces?

Ask the children to count across kinds of things. Make a display where on Monday there are vases to count, on Tuesday beads, on Wednesday books, and on Thursday and Friday a miscellany. Vary the display to make it novel and inviting, but always make sure the things for counting lie from left to right.

Monday's counting

Friday's counting

Activity 3: Counting lines, rows and clusters or groups
Once the children have a good grasp of counting from left to right, you can introduce counting a column and a cluster. Use a display board to mount things that children can count upwards and downwards. These could be soft toys, matchboxes – in fact, any items that you can attach to a backing board.

Count the boxes

How many teddies are having a balloon ride?

Look for naturally occurring clusters like the number of leaves on a twig, or birds on the bird-table. Point out everyday groups of things for counting, for example, fruit in a bowl, a handful of crayons, the flowers in a vase. Show the children patterns in which groups often appear, like the dots on a die. (See also the activities under Level 1 'Conservation'.)

Activity 4: One-to-one correspondence
Using the home-corner tea-set, the dolls' house tea-set or some crockery and cutlery borrowed from the kitchen, let the children practise setting table for their friends, or the dolls. Ask them to give each doll a plate, bowl, and so on.

The children could devise their own games like giving each friend a crayon, a badge, a skipping rope, a drink, or a letter to take home.

Activity 5: Counting at secondhand
From a small group of children, through discussion, gather counting information about themselves, including, for example, how many

people live in their house
pets they have (beware the 57 goldfish!)
sisters they have
Shredded Wheat® they eat
pairs of shoes they have
five-year-olds there are.

Collect pictures of kinds of things from magazines, catalogues and advertisements. Mount them and store them in transparent folders or large envelopes. The children can lay these out to count. You can also ask them to search for, cut out and count collections of their own. Display your pictures and theirs in a 'counting corner'. Note that the children are not using numerals yet.

Activity 6: Counting rhymes
To reinforce the pattern of words used in number, teach the children some rhymes; for example, 'One, two, three, four, five, once I caught a fish alive', 'This old man', 'One, two, buckle my shoe', 'One finger, one thumb, keep moving'. Make up some with the children. For example, 'One, two, listen and do; three, four, sit on the floor; Kevin, please will you shut the door?' will have much appeal for Kevin and his friends.

teacher's drawings
cut-outs from magazines
child's drawings
magazine pictures
photos

Count the pictures

NOTATION AND RECORDING THE SIZE OF COUNTS

Commentary
When children start recording numbers, both they and their parents may feel that real mathematics is just beginning. This is probably because in the past computational skills have been seen as the most important part of maths. However, it is important to combat the pressures of the 'pages of sums' approach and continue to let the children work practically as much as possible. They could probably master all they need to know about the numbers one to ten without writing down anything, but reading and writing soon start to affect progress in number work. Practice in reading and writing, including that done during maths sessions, is important.

The first step is to give the children the idea that recording the number of a count can help us to remember it, so that we can replicate it or use it for further work. For example, we write down how many pints of milk are on order, so that we know what to order next week if we find we had too much or too little (assisting memory), and so that we can check our milk bill (further work, in this case computation).

We have included one activity on 'pairs'. Because so much about us is paired, the concept is used frequently. This is an example of a word in common use having a relationship with mathematical ideas.

Activity 1: Numerals attached to counts
When the children are competent at counting aloud, having had plenty of practice, introduce the numerals. Here are several activities to do on a 'one' day. Follow up with reinforcement/consolidation activities and then repeat some of the tasks for 'two', 'three', 'four', and so on. Ask the children to:

● Draw themselves, one balloon, one lollipop, one cake, and so on
● Put out a range of containers and put one item in each
● Mount and display a range of pictures each with a single item in them.

Now you have a variety of 'ones' to attach a numeral to. First, draw a number '1' on the board, on a piece of paper with a paintbrush or in the sandtray, making sure that all the children are in a position to see that a '1' is drawn as a vertical line, starting at the top.

Get the children to pretend they each have a 'magic' finger and draw 1s in the air. Now let the children go round the pictures and draw magic 1s on each. Then, letting them work individually, give them a supply of little labels each with the numeral 1 on them. They can attach the numerals to things around the classroom. This is their first record of a counting exercise.

Activity 2: Numerals in sequence
Arrange a counting table or display like those in the 'Beginning counting' activities above. Let the children have turns and watch while each does a series of counting exercises and matches the appropriate numeral.

Arrange a display which can be regularly and frequently changed over a period of weeks, to give the children opportunities to match numerals to the appropriate counts.

Activity 3: Beads in lines and rows
Ask the children to thread a number of beads on a string. They can match a numeral to each of the beads, laying the beads first horizontally and then vertically.

Activity 4: Putting a numeral to actual counts

Let the children write, trace, paint, draw, colour and make the shapes of the numeral which matches their actual counts. So, if they lay six shells in a sand tray, they can draw '6' in the sand. If they make a model bird with three feathers in its tail, they can do a seed trail to make a numeral '3' to attach to the tail.

Activity 5: Matching numerals to pictures

Encourage the children to record how many trees, windows, clouds, etc. there are in their own pictures and in pictures you provide.

Copymasters **1** (Numeral–set match) and **2–4** (Counting and recording counts) present some exercises in counting and matching.

Activity 6: Number lines

On cardboard strips marked off in ten equal sections, write in, or let the children write in, the numerals. Set a number of objects along the line, and say how many altogether. Let the children count groups or sets of objects and check their counts by matching them against the number line.

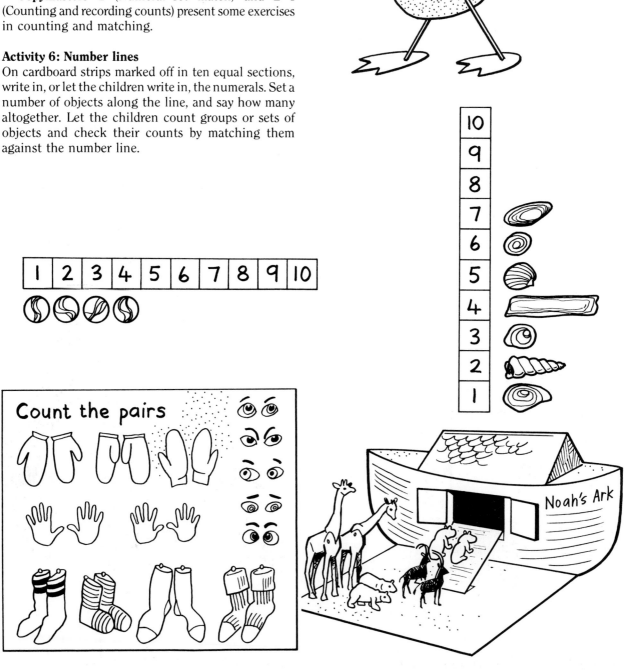

Activity 7: Pairs

Two socks are not a pair unless they match. The notion of 'pair' seems to carry with it a connection beyond 'twoness'. In fact, it would seem that to talk of a pair engages with two mathematical ideas, namely the number and the membership of a set. Discuss the pairs to be seen on human beings, including pairs of eyes, ears, legs and hands, and give the children work on pairs as well as the work on the number 'two'.

Copymaster **5** (Pairs) reinforces some of this work.

10

CARDINAL AND ORDINAL NUMBERS

Commentary
Children need to understand that saying something is *eighth* in a row is a different use of the number 'eight' than saying that there are *eight* objects in a group. For example, when we say, 'There are five boats in the row', 'five' is a cardinal number. If we say, 'The fourth boat has a flag', we are using ordinal number. But if we were to ask for four boats, this is not asking for the fourth boat! Cardinal number gives totals and subtotals, ordinal number position. Some children find the difference between a count and a position confusing. Help them by letting them master cardinal number thoroughly first, and by not mixing cardinal and ordinal number in the same problem.

Activity 1: Ordinal number
Now that the children can count and put cardinal numbers in sequence, you can give them opportunities to put things in order. First put some objects in order, such as soft toys at a model bus stop or play food for a giant's breakfast. Then discuss who is second in the bus queue, or what is the fifth thing the giant is going to eat for breakfast. Let the children come and point to a toy or item and say its position.

Let the children create their own ordered rows, including runners or boats past a finishing line in a race, children in a line at hometime, and clothes they take off (or put on) for PE.

Activity 2: Ordinal number in stories and rhymes
Look for and point out ordinal numbers in stories. For example: 'The children had three wishes. What was their first wish?' 'What were the first, second and third sons given by their father?'

Activity 3: Recording ordinal number
When the children have practised naming the order of things and labelling them, they can work at recording their ordering, and complete work set out in their books on ordering.
Copymaster 6 (Ordinal numbers) is a sample sheet of ideas.

THE LANGUAGE OF NUMBER

Commentary

While in many senses mathematics is a language in its own right, communication of mathematical ideas is usually through spoken or written language. This means that words in common use may have a special meaning in a mathematical setting, which can lead to confusion for children. We need to be constantly alert for misunderstandings of language rather than of the mathematics. Some examples of areas prone to language complications are these:

● Numbers are used in making comparisons. The vocabulary used in measurement is relevant here. We say we need *more* bottles of milk on Saturday and *more* material for a longer skirt. Children need to know that 7 is *more than* 5, but *less than* 8. Through your use of appropriate vocabulary, the children will begin to use it too.

● The existence of '0' in the number system is of vital importance, but we call it a variety of names. These include 'zero', 'nought', 'nil', and 'nothing'. Of these, 'nothing' is probably the least helpful and is mathematically inaccurate. But whatever your choice of word, it helps to be consistent and to elaborate the meaning through regular explanations. (The children will meet '0' at Number Level 3.)

● We need to be aware of language and cultural differences. For example, in English single words identify whole numbers up to and including 20; in French word combinations are used from 17 to 19.

Activity 1: Words for numbers

Introduce children to number rhymes in books and to counting books where the number has been written as a word as well as a numeral. Make a class number book to ten, or let each child make their own.

A number book

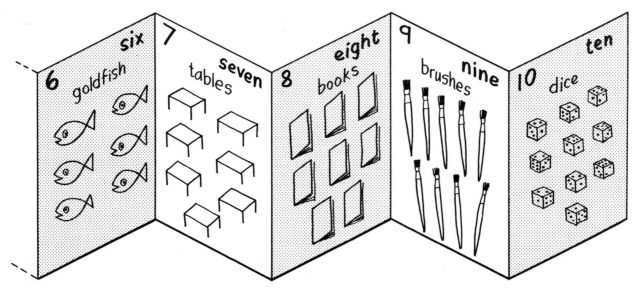

12

Put a number chart on the wall, and let the children count as a group, reading from the chart. Cover the numerals sometimes, and let them have turns at reading the number words or pointing them out to the group.

flap can be put down over numerals

flap can be put down over number words

Activity 2: Responding to words for numbers

Make some flash cards, each with a number word from 'one' to 'ten' on it. Use these in giving instructions. For example, in PE, hold up a card with 'two' written on it, say 'Hop' and the children have to give two hops; hold up 'six' and say 'Step' and the children have to take six steps; and so on. In music, you could give instructions to percussion players and to children clapping using number flash cards. Another possibility is to include instructions on the board or in their books which say, for example, 'Draw two things you like to eat.' 'Find three books about dogs.'

Collect favourite numbers and information about numbers, and record number information about the children themselves on a number display or in a number book. Add some more 'abstract' numbers, including the number of days in a week, seasons in a year and so on. Use both numerals and number words, to ensure the children can use both with facility.

Activity 3: Language in maths
While the children are counting, you can begin to use words they will need in making comparisons. Here are a selection of words that can be introduced:

> more than/less than
> the same as
> most/least
> low/lower/lowest
> high/higher/highest

A *Words for Numbers* book can be made for the children to consult. This should include concepts that the children have already met, such as 'pairs' and 'sets'.

 is more than

Make display cards with entries like 'is more than', 'is less than'. Ask the children to practise making number sentences, using their counts and the numeral cards.

Activity 4: Matching and comparing
Let the children match two sets of items, using pieces of string or wool to join each item to its fellow in the other set. They can then say whether one set has more or less than the other.

Which has more ?

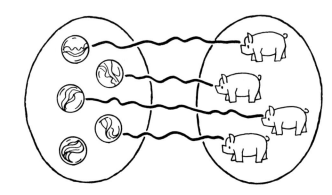

C7–12, R1

CONSERVATION GAMES

Commentary
You will be able to observe whether individual children are beginning to conserve number, when they add to a count they have started and are confident about counting on, without going back to the beginning.

To conserve, they should recognise that a counted set is the same, no matter how the individual objects are arranged.

Number games can be played at all stages in children's mathematical development. We have put dice games under 'Conservation' because a die can present a pattern of 'three', for example, in a number of ways. Here are some:

Dice with dots on them can be used to test conservation, while numeral dice help consolidate number recognition. Some toy shops sell loose dice with varying numbers of sides, enabling children to show their understanding of conservation beyond six.

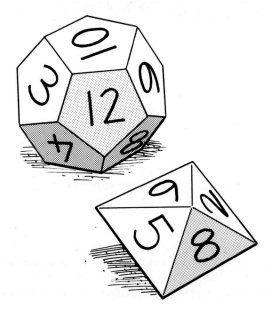

Activity 1: Let's conserve

In a group, give each child a toy, or marble or brick, letting the children count as you go. Ask how many there are altogether. Then distribute the same items unevenly around the group, omitting some children and giving others several items. Ask how many altogether. Vary this again and again until all the children are convinced that the number of objects is always the same. Play with a set of Unifix® or oranges or something else to count, moving them about to make different patterns, and quiz the children each time about how many there are altogether. They can record their observations, construct their own patterns of a number and record them.

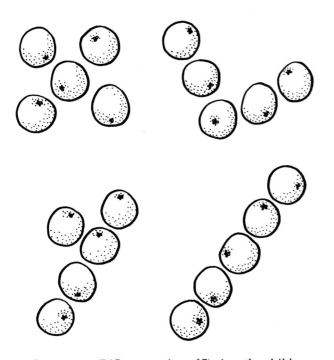

Copymaster 7 (Conservation of 5) gives the children a chance to record some work on number patterns.

Copymaster 8 (Conservation of 2, 3, 5) depicts dominoes. Encourage the children to look at the patterns on whole dominoes as well as those on each half.

Activity 2: Dice games

Let the children play track games on boards without numbers, to consolidate their recognition and conservation of number to 10. Start with a blank die, or cardboard spinner, on which you write configurations of two and three dots. **Resource copymaster R1** (Spinners) may be useful here.

The game on **copymaster 9** (Ladybird race) can be played with a die or spinner.

The games on **copymasters 10** (Cheese chase) and **11** (Home-time!) can be played with a die with any pattern of numbers on them. **Copymaster 12** (Aliens) is a die/numeral recognition game to 6 for two players; the players throw the die in turn, colouring a section of the alien that matches the die score.

Activity 3: Card games

A conventional pack of cards has number sequences to 10 in each suit, but the numbers are inverted at the bottom of each card. Instead, make your own pack using dots rather than numerals. You could have as many suits (by colour or shape of dots) as you like.

The children could play a memory game with the cards. Shuffle the cards and spread out face down. Let each child turn up two cards to try for a matching pair.

The children could also play 'Snap'.

ESTIMATION

Commentary

Estimates are informed guesses. As soon as the children are beginning to conserve small numbers, you can encourage them to estimate before they count.

Estimation is a very important mathematical skill, especially where a problem has an answer (and there may be more than one). When you work through a problem, whether it is the quantity of wallpaper needed to paper the living room or how long it will take to walk to town, you may use past experience at the start by making an informed guess. Then you check the guess by doing some computation and look at the match between your estimate and your answer to see if you have the right 'order' of outcome. If the arithmetic tells you it takes two hours to walk to town, and your estimate is 20 minutes, you know you need to try again! As we increasingly use calculators and computers

to assist computation, it becomes even more important to know what sort of answer to expect.

Activity 1: Play at estimating counts

The children may be familiar with challenges like guessing the number of sweets in a jar at the local fête. The problem is that this requires a wild guess. Play games like this with the children, but make sure that the answers do not exceed ten. For example, show the children a marble and a matchbox and ask them to estimate how many marbles will go in the matchbox. (If you do this with a small group, you could set out their estimates so that there are maths extension possibilities for another day – a simple bar chart, for example.) The estimates are then put to the test. Then question the children further to establish what the result would be if the marbles were slightly bigger, or the matchbox were bigger while the marbles stayed the same size.

Another possibility is to hold some shells in your open hand. Let the children look at them for about 5 seconds, and then ask for estimates. Put the estimates to the test.

Activity 2: Play at estimating measures

Give the children opportunities to make estimates in measurement, limiting the answers to ten or below. Here are some suggestions:

● How many exercise books cover your table?
● How many strides does it take to cross the classroom?
● How many 'feet' is it across the carpet?
● How many thumbs fit across the register?

● How many bricks will fit in the shoe box with its lid on?
● How many toy sheep will fit in the sheep pen (standing up)?

Activity 3: Estimating and calculators

Calculators are important tools and children should have opportunities very early on in their lives to use them in mathematical settings. Used as tally machines they can be very useful in estimating games. For example, show the children that calculators can be used to confirm or confound estimates. Let them do short and simple experiments. For example, ask them to estimate how many children in the group like trifle. They then use the calculator to total how many, by keying in +1 each time they get a 'yes' (see 'Beginning addition', Activity 1).

BEGINNING ADDITION

Commentary

Aim for 100% success. We need confident mathematicians! This will require taking the children forward a step at a time, because then you can pick up a problem the first time it occurs, and not have a child experience repeated failure.

It is important that you are able to oversee each child, so place the children in small ability groups with flexible membership.

As in 'Beginning counting', the children themselves are their own and your first resource.

In putting several more objects into a set, as in Activities 1 to 3 opposite, the children are in fact

adding two sets together – that is, the original set and however many more.

In setting out the first sets for them to combine, try to practise the left to right across the page layout, with the answer on the right. Not all sums are arranged like this, but much early number work depends on this kind of presentation. We do not want children to feel they do not understand maths simply because they do not understand the way it appears on the page.

There are lots of words in use in computation discussion. Use the words that you find familiar at first. Tell the children about the words you do not use regularly, when you feel they are ready.

Activity 1: And one more child makes . . .

From a group, name three children to stand up. Let the children count how many are standing. Ask another to stand and say '. . . and one more makes . . . ?' Do this again and again, getting the named children to sit down, stand on one leg, put their hands in the air, and so on. Then increase the number you add to the set, ensuring that the final total does not exceed ten. ('Estimation' Activity 3 has links with this activity.)

Activity 2: And one more thing makes . . .

Ask each child in a group to collect a given number of objects. Go around the group, asking how many objects each child has. From a handful of things that you have yourself, add one more to each set and say '. . . and one more makes . . . ?' Let each child assemble different numbers of things in their 'set', and play this out many times. Let each child have a go as 'teacher' while you become a member of the group.

Some traditional stories are useful here, for the children can count '. . . and one more makes . . .' as each person is added to the story.

Repeat the activity many times, adding a greater number of items to each set, but ensuring the final set size does not go above ten. The children can take turns at displaying their counts, and what happens when one more is added.

Activity 3: Recording

Give the children pictures on which to match, draw and record additions to sets.

Activity 4: Putting sets together

Let the children lay out two separate sets, count each, and then physically combine them to give a total count. Play with a group, doing this several times yourself, and then letting each child have a go.

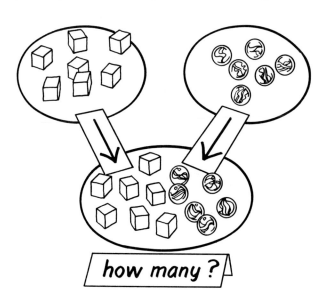

Activity 5: Practical addition

Let children make up their own collections of objects which they count and combine. Remember to give them chances to add more than two small sets. You can limit their choices by supplying numerals on cards of different colours. The children choose numerals of different colours, collect those numbers of objects, and then combine the sets, finding the numeral corresponding to the count of the combined sets.

Activity 6: Addition language

Here are some of the words children need to know, even if they do not use them themselves: 'addition', 'add', 'plus', 'the sum of', 'total', 'makes'. There is also much language they will have met during earlier counting activities, including: 'more', 'most', 'less', 'least', 'bigger', 'smaller', and so on. Encourage the children to talk about numbers using this vocabulary. Use these words in displays, flashcards and work tasks.

FIRST ADDITIONS

Commentary

When you are preparing maths work with non-maths words in it, give the children a picture–word code sheet. They should then have a chance to do the maths rather than spending all their time trying to find out what the words mean!

Activity 1: Picture recording

Let the children assemble two sets of things and put the two sets together, as in 'Beginning addition' above, then ask them to draw in their books what they did. When they can record what they have done practically, you can give them some picture recording problems which are partly drawn already.

Activity 2: Addition

Give the children additions with words like 'plus' or 'add' and 'equals' in them. For example:

● 4 cats add 2 cats equals ___ cats altogether.
● 3 oranges plus 1 orange makes ___ oranges.

The children should do plenty of these, using all combinations of number to ten. Include some like this:

● 1 sock add 4 socks add 5 socks makes ___ socks.

You can draw pictures to make these more inviting, but the children should use counting aids as and when they need them. All the objects for the count do not have to be drawn in.

18

BEGINNING SUBTRACTION

Commentary

You may choose to wait until the children are competent at addition before introducing subtraction. You could do both operations alongside one another, or subtraction first if you wish. The important point is that addition and subtraction are related, and the children should be helped to understand this.

It could be argued that subtraction is more familiar to young children because they have plenty of experience of having things 'taken away' from them before they reach school age! However, what they may not have a sense of is the connection between 'take aways' and 'adds'. For example: $2 + 3 = 5$, $5 - 2 = 3$, $5 - 3 = 2$.

Once more it is important to remember aspects of language: 'take away', 'minus', 'less than' and so on.

Activity 1: Take me away!

From a group, ask a number of children to stand at the front. Count how many there are and then physically take one child away, and ask how many are left. Do this repeatedly with different participants, taking two away, then three, eventually trying all patterns of take away possible with the group.

Activity 2: Take away objects

Repeat Activity 1 using things belonging to the children, for example, PE bags, pumps, cardigans, shoes, pencil cases and other things available. Then work with things around the room, and pictures of things.

take away 1   how many left ?

Activity 3: Take away strips

Using rubber stamp pictures, those you have drawn yourself, or some cut from a catalogue, make a series of pictures along a strip of card. Make little cuts between the pictures so that they can be flapped up and down.

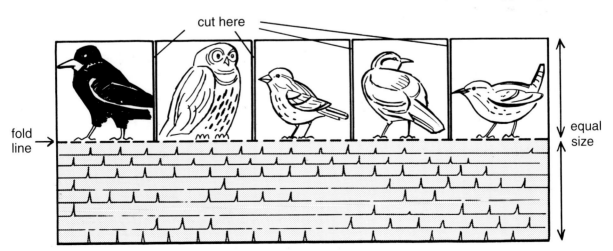

cut here

fold line →

equal size

Use the strips with the children to play take aways, setting up the starting number of birds on the wall or buns in the shop, or whatever the pictures depict. Flap down out of sight the number taken away, and count those left. If you find it helpful, you could make a large take away strip, to use with a group of children.

Copymaster 13 (Take away strips) provides two ready made examples.

Activity 4: Take away rhymes

Teach the children songs and rhymes like 'Ten green bottles', 'Five speckled frogs', 'Five little ducks went swimming one day', 'There were ten in the bed', 'Poor Jane Higgins, she had five piggins' and 'Five little monkeys walked along the shore'. Make a copy of some rhymes in a homemade book for the book corner.

FIRST SUBTRACTIONS

Commentary

Take care with the concept of subtraction! People often see subtraction as being about taking away or about the difference between two things. There are both language difficulties bound up in these concepts and a difference in direction between the two views. 'Less than' implies a 'more to less' direction, but the difference notion can be described as being in either direction.

In the children's experience, for example in corner shops, many adults solve subtractions by adding on. This is an important approach and one which you need to be aware of in giving the children the vocabulary of subtraction. But beware of too narrow an adherence to standard methods! It is important for the children to be able to offer personal methods too. Explanations of personal methods are often good ways of exploring underlying concepts.

Activity 1: Practical take aways

As in 'Beginning addition' Activity 5 and 'First additions' Activity 1 above, the children should now set up their own take aways, laying out a number of toys, picture recording how many, and then actually taking some away to find how many left, and drawing them.

Activity 2: Subtraction language

Discuss with the children the words used in talking about 'take aways', including 'subtract', 'minus' and 'take'. Make up a group take away story, and display a picture version.

Activity 3: Subtraction

Give the children written subtractions with words like 'take away' and 'left over' written in. For example:

- 6 carrots take away 1 carrot. ___ carrots left over.
- 9 mice take away 5 mice leaves ___ mice.

As with additions at this stage, pictures will make the subtractions more inviting, but the children should use counting aids as and when they need them. All the objects at the start or finish do not need to be drawn in.

20

NUMBERS IN PLAY

Commentary

The best arena for children to do real counting is provided by role play games in the classroom. There are many possible settings for this work. We suggest a few here and will develop these at AT 2 Number Levels 2 and 3.

Activity 1: Play house

In the home corner, create a one-roomed house. It could be the house for the following:

● The three bears (counting, one-to-one correspondence, sequencing)
● Red Riding Hood's grandma (First Red Riding Hood says, 'My, what big ears . . .' etc., ordinal number)
● A 'real' family (number on house, knocks at the door, counting in the cupboard – numbers of cups, plates, etc.; setting the table – one-to-one correspondence; dressing the baby doll – ordinal number).

Activity 2: Play shop

The play house can become a shop, with a table inside, set against the open window as a counter. Fill the till or cash box with play coins and exchange single items for a coin. The children can count the items and count the coins. Try letting the children play with these:

● Play dough fruits or cakes (a recipe for this dough is in 'Resourcing your mathematics' at the beginning of the book)
● Paper hats
● Play lollipops
● Old greeting cards.

Theme play shops are suggested in Number Level 2.

Activity 3: Play post office

This kind of play shop has much potential. Try:

● Sticky labels with a picture drawn on them as stamps
● Old postcards and greeting cards
● Parcel string
● Gift tags.

Activity 4: Play telephone

A strong cardboard box like those used for dishwashers or cookers makes a good kiosk. When painted and decorated, set up an old phone or a play phone in it. Put in a box with a slot for coins, and a list of important phone numbers.

Activity 5: Play hospital

Create a doctor's bag with equipment. Let the children set out the 'ward' of beds (boxes) with toys or child patients and solve problems like:

● How many beds do six patients need (one-to-one correspondence)?

● If two patients came in today and there were three already, how many altogether (practical addition)?
● How many bandages are needed for two arms and two legs (counting/addition)?
● Teddy Growl is going home, how many patients will be left (practical subtraction)?

Activity 6: Play spaceship

This needs more setting up than the others, though an upended table with a sheet over it and cone of silver foil covered card on top will do. Supply the astronauts with helmets – large cereal packets with holes cut for the face and foil covering are adequate. Also supply the following:

● A flight log to fill in (counting and sequencing)
● A countdown chart
● A picture route map (sequencing).

21

REVIEW: NUMBER SO FAR

The children should now have a good grounding in numbers to 10. They should feel as enlivened by the prospect of number work as they are by any other activity they do in school, including drawing, singing and PE!

The foundations of mathematical work and the children's appreciation of their ability to see and describe the world mathematically is an essential outcome of early number work. We often hear discussions of the need for a return to basics, but this is often equated with computational skill of a very narrow kind. We must not allow children to narrow their focus on number to 'sums'. The important areas of work that we envisage at this level are:

Counting
Learning some of the language of number
Beginning recording
Cardinal and ordinal numbers
Conservation
Estimation
Early addition and subtraction
Seeing numbers in active, real and practical contexts.

Attainment Target 2: Number, Level 2

Pupils should understand and use number, including estimation and approximation, interpreting results and checking for reasonableness.

Programme of study	Statements of attainment	Examples
Pupils should engage in activities which involve:	Pupils should be able to:	Pupils could:
• knowing and using addition and subtraction facts up to 10. • reading, writing and ordering numbers to at least 100 and using the knowledge that the 10s digit indicates the number of 10s.	a) Demonstrate that they know and can use number facts, including addition and subtraction.	*Know that if six pencils are taken from a box of ten there will be four left.* *Know that if two dice show 'three' and 'five' then the total is eight.*
• solving whole-number problems involving addition and subtraction, including money. • comparing two numbers to find the difference. • using coins in simple contexts.	b) Solve whole-number problems involving addition and subtraction.	*Work out the change from 20p when two biscuits costing 5p and 7p are purchased.* *Choose correct coins to pay 34p for an item in the class shop.*
• understanding the meaning of 'a half' and 'a quarter'.	c) Identify halves and quarters.	*Find a quarter of a length of string.* *Know that half of eight is four.*
• using non-standard measures in length, area, capacity, 'weight' and time; comparing objects and events and recognising the need for standard units. • learning and using the language for common units in length, capacity, 'weight', and time (e.g. m, $\frac{1}{2}$m, l, $\frac{1}{2}$l, kg, $\frac{1}{2}$kg, day, hour, half-hour).	d) Recognise the need for standard units of measurement.	*Suggest things which are commonly measured in metres, miles, litres, pints, pounds, hours.*

ADDITION AND SUBTRACTION

Commentary

Teachers often let children use workcards and work-sheets to do pages of 'sums'. There are some points to consider.

● Why are the children doing these calculations?
● Are patterns in number preserved, where possible, in the order the calculations are presented?
● Are the workcards and worksheets ideal in layout and condition? (We have all seen children working on sheets that make little sense to the teacher, let alone the children, and using workcards that are 15 years old, and look it.)

It may be that many children become disinterested in maths when they are forced to rehearse skills they already have. They consequently spend less time on those aspects of maths that are so useful in everyday life, like estimation, approximation and problem solving. In this respect it is necessary to look at how schemes are being used. It is the teacher and the children who should set the mathematics agenda, not the writers of a scheme. Schemes are not substitutes for school development plans, they are resources which should be employed as and when necessary. There is nothing more destructive of children's mathematical development than to make them work through a scheme regardless of individual strengths and insights!

There is a need here to be clear about the previous experiences of the children. If they are moving to Level 2 work within the year, then you should find this no problem. However, if this represents a transition of

class as well as year, then it is important to establish what the child knows in terms of their language experience.

At Level 2, symbols are used as 'shorthand' for important mathematical operations and relationships. It is important to be consistent in using these, while still allowing children to develop personal methods for problem solution.

Activity 1: Addition: the 'plus' and 'equals' signs

Discuss with the children the signs for 'add' and 'equals'. Give them numeral cards and some with '+' or '=', and watch them make the start of a calculation and transfer it to their books. This activity should be used as a bridge from Level 1 work.

$$\boxed{2} \; \boxed{+} \; \boxed{5} \; \boxed{=} \; \boxed{}$$

$$\boxed{1} \; \boxed{+} \; \boxed{} \; \boxed{=} \; \boxed{4}$$

Activity 2: Additions

Now that the children have met all the appropriate vocabulary and know what to expect, they should be given plenty of opportunities to record additions to ten. Both layout and vocabulary should be varied in the presentation of the calculations.

$$7 + 1 = \square$$

$$8 + 2 = \square$$

$$5 + 5 = \square$$

$$4 + \square = 5$$

$$\square + 1 = 6$$

$$\begin{array}{cc} 4\,+ & 3\,+ \\ 2 & 3 \\ \hline \\ \hline \end{array}$$

$$\begin{array}{cc} 2\,+ & 6\,+ \\ 7 & 3 \\ \hline \\ \hline \end{array}$$

2 add 3 makes $\square$

5 plus 4 equals $\square$

make 10

add 4 and ____

2 and ____

23

Activity 3: Addition dice games
When playing track games like 'Snakes and ladders', to make the game move quickly and reinforce number bonds, the children could play with two dice with the 6 deleted (so that totals do not exceed ten), summing the two numbers before they make a move. Use commercial track games and those you make yourself. Make dice or spinners which use the numbers 6 to 9. For example, the children could play with a pair of spinners, where one has 3 to 8 and the other has 1s and 2s. (**Resource copymaster R1** includes blank spinners for you to use here.)

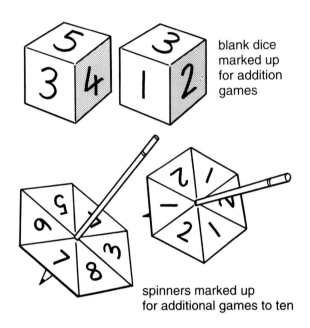

blank dice marked up for addition games

spinners marked up for additional games to ten

There are track games on **copymasters 14** (Leap frog) and **15** (Planes and parachutes).

Activity 4: Addition card games
Make some addition games, using, for example, bonds to five or ten. The game can be like 'Bingo' or simply a set of cards with numbers on them which an individual or two children can assemble into patterns of five or ten.

The games for two players on **copymasters 16** (Make five) and **17** (Make ten) can be used in this way. Photocopy each copymaster on to card, and cut out the game cards. Share the cards between the players. In 'Make five', the players take turns to put down cards which make a total of five in any combination. In 'Make ten', they take turns to make patterns of ten (six and four etc.). For both games the winner is the player with fewest (or no) cards left.

Activity 5: Addition using a calculator
Let the children check their answers to additions by using a calculator. Then ask them to make up additions on the calculator and write them out with the answers. They can give the additions to friends to do, without letting them see the answers.

Activity 6: Subtraction: the 'minus' and 'equals' signs
Discuss with the children the signs for '−' and '=' (they have already met the equals sign in addition). Make cards with the minus sign on them and use them with the cards for Activity 1 'Addition: the "plus" and "equals" signs'. Let the children set out a subtraction using numeral cards and the sign cards before transferring it to their book.

Activity 7: Subtractions
The children should have plenty of opportunity to record subtractions to ten. Both layout and vocabulary should be varied in the presentation of subtractions.

$$8 - 4 = \square$$
$$7 - 3 = \square$$
$$10 - 2 = \underline{}$$
$$6 - \square = 2$$
$$\square - 1 = 7$$

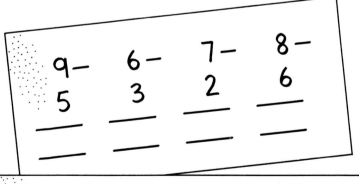

$$9- \quad 6- \quad 7- \quad 8-$$
$$5 \quad\quad 3 \quad\quad 2 \quad\quad 6$$

7 take away 4 leaves $\square$

5 minus 2 equals $\square$

3 subtract 1 equals ___

The difference between 5 and 2 is ___

24

Activity 8: Dice games
Let the children play track games using two dice. Before they move, they subtract the smaller number from the bigger number shown on the dice or spinners. Vary the spinners and dice, so that the children can practise all subtraction possibilities, within 10.

The track games on **copymasters 14** (Leap frog) and **15** (Planes and parachutes) may be adapted in this way.

blank dice marked up
for subtraction games

blank die marked
up 5, 6, 7, 8, 9, 10

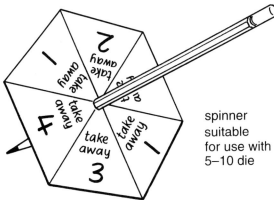

spinner
suitable
for use with
5–10 die

Activity 9: Subtraction using a calculator
As in Activity 5, 'Addition using a calculator', let the children check their answers using a calculator, and then set subtractions for their friends, using the calculator to mark answers.

Activity 10: Oral work on number bonds
When you have a couple of minutes with the class, between sessions or activities, give them some quick-fire oral work. For example:

● Let's make 5. What do I need to make 5? 1 and what? 2 and what?

● Let's make 10. 7 and what? 9 and what? 1 and 4 and what?

● The answer I want is 2. I have 8 buns. How many must I eat to have only 2 left? What if I start with 3 buns?

● I start with 5 marbles. If I lose 2, how many are left?

Activity 11: Think of a number
Give the children a number, for example, 26. Go around the class, asking what can they tell you about that number. You may get things like:

● It is written 2 and 6.
● It has 2 tens.
● The other way round it would be 62.
● $2 + 6 = 8$, $6 + 2 = 8$, $6 - 2 = 4$.
● My birthday is 26 May.
● My mum is 26.
● My cousin lives at number 26.
● 2 is a swan swimming and 6 is a swan sleeping.
● There are 26 letters in the alphabet.

Now let the children choose a number and investigate it in a small group setting.

NUMBER PATTERNS TO 100

C9–11,14–15, R2–4

Commentary
Mathematics is about patterns. Much of the fun to be found in maths is in the patterns that occur and that we can make with numbers, or through using numbers. Many adults who feel they are no good at maths are people who have never been shown that patterns in maths are as beautiful as patterns in language and art. It is important to say this because a liking or disliking for maths is in the hands of teachers of young children. It is vital that the children and their parents begin to see that maths is not just 'sums' and sometimes has little to do with sums.

Activity 1: Making patterns
Make patterns of numbers up to and including ten, with Unifix® or Multilink®, sticky shapes, a ten by ten square drawn on large squared paper, or beads on a string. If the children have good hand control skills, they could draw graphs of number bonds to ten.

Resource copymaster R4 is a page of large squares.

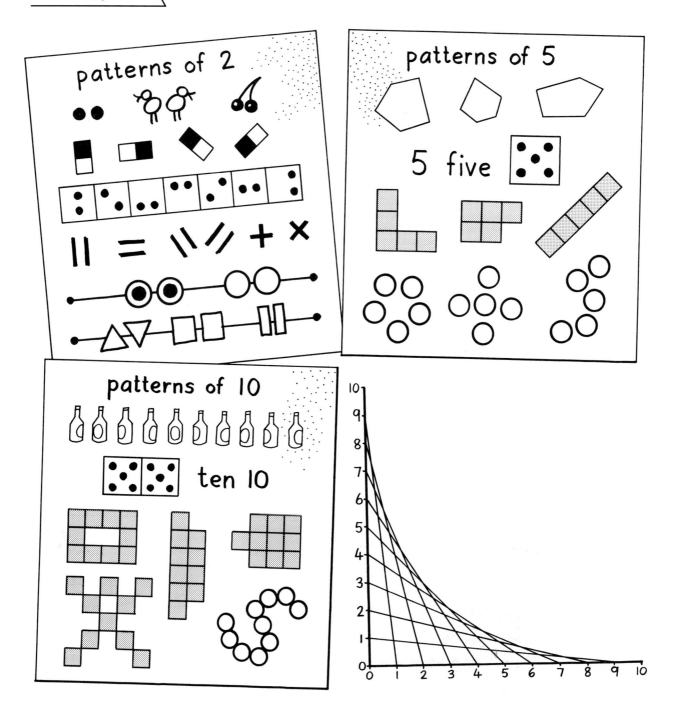

Activity 2: Inventing patterns

Ask the children to create patterns which involve counting to ten. Some of these may demonstrate bonds to ten. Encourage the children to devise short ways of describing the patterns they create, using maths symbols. Here are some possibilities.

Activity 3: Oral counting

Here are games to play with a group or the whole class in a spare few minutes. Let all the children count aloud up to 10, up to 20, up to 30, . . . and eventually up to 100.

Then start the counts at numbers other than 1, like this: 'Count from 26 to 43', 'Count from 17 to 52'.

Make the game more complicated by saying things like: 'I want you to count together, up to 40. Each time you say a number which is written with a '1' in it, clap your hands.' The first twelve numbers will be like this:

1 (clap), 2, 3, 4, 5, 6, 7, 8, 9, 10 (clap), 11 (clap), 12 (clap), . . .

Next introduce clapping for '3s' then '5s'.

Keep the counting short and snappy, for the children will soon get in a muddle if their concentration breaks. When they are good at counting as a class, ask some to listen while other small groups or pairs do the counting.

Try asking the children to say aloud the answers to questions like the following:

● What is the next number after 16?
● What is one more than 74?
● What is two more than 11?
● Which is the bigger number, 23 or 12?
● Which is smaller, 78 or 87?
● Which is biggest, 33, 45 or 56?
● Which is smallest, 2, 15 or 10?

Activity 4: Play with 100

Play counting in tens, counting backwards in tens, and colouring hundred squares in a variety of ways. The hundred square is a device that can be returned to again and again, in cyclical fashion, as the children master place value, and begin to work with larger numbers.

Here is a typical sequence of tasks for a child to do, over a period of days or weeks:

● Colour the pattern of counting in ones (that is, every square!).
● Colour the pattern of counting in tens.
● Colour all the numbers with a 3 in them (or 4, or any digit).
● Fill in the numbers on a blank ten by ten square.
● Fill in the numbers on a blank ten by ten square and then colour the important numbers to them. (They may include their age, the number of brothers and sisters they have, the number of their house and so on.)

The purpose here is to encourage the children to play around with the hundred square until they are thoroughly familiar with it. Note that the patterns of two, five, and other numbers will be considered at Level 3, where the hundred square can be used again.

There are hundred squares on **resource copymasters R2** and **R3**.

Activity 5: Counting games

Let the children play games like 'Snakes and ladders', which is actually a number track and not a hundred square, but nevertheless will get them looking at and calling out numbers to 100. You (or the children) can invent other track games.

There are unnumbered track games on **copymasters 9** (Ladybird race), **10** (Cheese chase) and **11** (Home time!) and numbered ones on **copymasters 14** (Leap frog) and **15** (Planes and parachutes).

HOW MANY TENS?

Commentary

Place value is fundamental to all number work. In order for children to manipulate numbers they must appreciate that, for example, the symbol '1' can mean a single unit, or one ten, or one hundred, or one million million!

Young children have a fascination with numbers. They often count, out loud, whole sequences of numbers – trying to get to one hundred is a common game. However, children's ability to learn the words used to describe natural numbers should not be confused with an understanding of place value. Being able to say 'twenty-three' and even write down '23' cannot be taken as evidence that the number twenty-three is understood in terms of its constitutents and the conventions used in writing it.

Activity 1: What's in a number?

The children will need a large number of counting aids for this activity. Unifix®, Multilink® or Cuisenaire® ones and tens, or spent matches and elastic bands, are ideal. The way you do this activity will depend on what aids are available.

First show the children that a number of Unifix®, say 34, can be put in a pile, or fixed end to end. Then explain that numbers are grouped so that they are easier to work with and that they are put in groups of ten. The outcome is like this:

3 tens **4** units

3   **4**

34 'Unifix'

Lay the assembled real Unifix® on a piece of card with large numerals '3' and '4' written as 34. Tell the children if nobody spots it, that there are 3 tens where the 3 is and 4 ones where the 4 is.

Try this again and again for different numbers. Then let the children lay out numbers of their own choice. (Give them an upper limit or you will run out of Unifix® or Multilink®!)

Activity 2: Recording what's in a number
Let the children repeat Activity 1, and transfer their findings to their books. Drawing a tower of ten can be a problem for some children. A stencil may help.

15 Multilink · 25 Multilink

I ten **5** units   **2** tens **5** units

SOLVING PROBLEMS AND 'FINDING THE DIFFERENCE'

C18

Commentary
If you give the children the sums $6 + 3$ and $3 + 6$, they may do them independently and not make connections between them. Children get used to the idea of 'one sum at a time', and then fail to recognise that addition is commutative, that is:

$$6 + 3 = 3 + 6$$

Once they know this, they will commonly begin to tackle addition by taking the bigger number first, no matter how the sum is presented. They will do $2 + 8$ as though it were $8 + 2$, because it seems easier *and* gives the same answer.

As well as getting to grips with commutativity, children also need to understand the associativity of addition. For example, they need to understand that

$$(3 + 6) + 4 = 3 + (6 + 4)$$

and that the right-hand version is a lot easier to handle in this particular example!

While addition is commutative, subtraction is not.

$$6 - 3 \neq 3 - 6 \quad (\neq \text{ means does not equal})$$

Nor is subtraction associative.

$$(9 - 6) - 3 \neq 9 - (6 - 3)$$

Children need both to understand commutativity and associativity, and to know where each is applicable.

Play situations at this level are ideal arenas to develop children's computation skills in practical problem-solving situations.

Activity: Mix and match
Give the children additions and subtractions in mixed exercises. Discuss the configurations of numbers, the ways of tackling calculations by, for example, starting with the larger number in additions and the larger number in subtractions (which can be done no other way at this stage).

A single sample page of these problems is presented on **copymaster 18** (Add and subtract).

The children should now be ready to tackle number problems like those that can be presented in the class shop, or other play situations. Look, for example, at 'Number play at Level 2', Activity 2.

SHOPPING

Commentary

Shopping is familiar to every child. However, that does not necessarily mean they understand how the system works. We have a suggested discussion list here, which should take the children from the idea of 'swopping' to an understanding of equivalence.

Activity 1: Swopping

Investigate things known to have been used in barter, and let the children act out explorers swopping beads for rubber, fruit, and other exotic things. Pirates could swop new masts or flags for jewels. Create a barter system especially for the class, where yogurt pots, stickers or conkers become sought after, and the medium of exchange.

We still barter with one another. Discuss with the children the idea that we might give our neighbours some of our pears, and hope for some apples from the neighbour's tree in return.

Activity 2: Spending

Use a classroom shop (as discussed in 'Number play at Level 2') and shopping games, to enable the children to practise spending money. Begin with 1p coins, and gradually introduce others.

There is a page of money equivalence problems on **copymaster 19** (Equivalence).

Activity 3: Change

When children understand equivalence and are adept at simple mental addition and subtraction they will be able to begin working on giving change. Let them try it in the classroom shop, and on paper.

Copymaster 20 (Change) has some shopping problems.

Activity 4: Bills

In the classroom shop (or restaurant, see 'Number play at Level 2') the children can begin to write down a list of items, add up the total cost, and then check their answers on the calculator.

A HALF AND A QUARTER

Commentary

The idea of 'halving' is probably familiar to children. They have probably all had to share a cake or a drink with another child at some time. However, it cannot be assumed that because they use 'half' and 'quarter' in everyday speech, they have a concept of what it means. Work on 'division' comes in Level 3, but you can lay the foundations for it by doing practical sharing into halves and quarters now.

Activity 1: Sharing half each

Make a number of play items, in sections so that they can be 'cut' into two, or four. For example, foam rubber sheeting makes sponge cakes, corrugated card brown bread for sandwiches and play dough makes excellent jam tarts, sweets and other imaginary edibles. These have the advantage that they are relatively durable, and with care could last for more than one set of children.

Using two children or two toys demonstrate that sharing the sponge cake *equally* between them means that each will have a half. The sponge is the whole, and a portion is a half. Share other play edibles and encourage the children to identify each half. Give them each opportunities to have a go.

Show the children how to write the word 'half' and the '$\frac{1}{2}$' sign. (The division sign is explained in 'First divisions', Activity 2 at Level 3.)

Then show the children how to share a quantity of, for example, rice or pasta.

Activity 2: Sharing quarter each

As in Activity 1, share play items between four children or toys, and let the children have goes at doing the same.

Show the children how to write a 'quarter' and the $\frac{1}{4}$ sign. Create a wallchart with this information on it. (Draw a quarter of the shape under the flaps.)

Activity 3: Paper folding halves and quarters

With a variety of kinds of paper and a range of tasks, get the children to cut shapes into halves and quarters.

Activity 4: Recording half and quarter

Ask the children to use the play edibles to create their own ways of sharing halves and quarters and draw

them in their books. Give the children additional recording that you have begun for them on worksheets or cards.

Copymasters **21** (Halves) and **22** (Quarters) give another method of presenting this work.

Make a half and quarter display, including a clock face, just showing a half and a quarter.

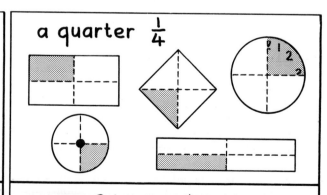

some puzzles
• half of your pocket money ?
• half of 10 pence ?
• half of 6 marbles ?
• halfway round the world – where is that ?

a game: Cut a paper shape into quarters.
Make each piece into something different.

 a $\frac{1}{4}$ of a square makes a

STARTING TO MEASURE

Commentary

The intention here is to give the children a wide range of practical experiences in measuring things themselves, and in beginning to record what they have measured.

The important point to get across to the children is that measuring has to be done carefully.

Estimation is as important in measurement as it is in number work. Note that estimation involving liquids can be more difficult than work with solids.

Activity 1: Handspans, cubits, feet and strides

Show the children how to measure length using their own personal measures, for example, handspans, cubits, feet and strides. You may also wish to give the children practice in using thumbs, fingers, books, pencils, blocks and other things from the maths resource box to measure length (and breadth and height).

Discuss with the children the idea of choosing the unit used to measure, basing the decision on an estimate of the outcome. For example, we may choose to measure across a room in strides, rather than pencils.

Here are some suggestions for tasks to give the children and some of the possible measuring 'units' they may use:

● Room, carpet, corridor, number line – strides, paces, feet

● Cupboard, window, table, wallchart, curtains – handspans, cubits

● Books, charts, pictures – fingers, blocks, pencils.

Draw the children's attention to the fact that they do not all get the same answers in their measuring. Set out some of the measurements children have made as a resource/display.

Measuring the table

How many handspans ?

Cara	6
Richard	4
Stuart	3
Chris	5
Yvonne	4

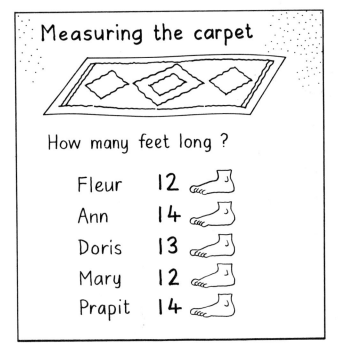

Measuring the carpet

How many feet long ?

Fleur	12
Ann	14
Doris	13
Mary	12
Prapit	14

Enliven the measurement tasks by doing a couple of tasks involving the whole class. For example, find out how many children need to lie head to toe to fit across the hall, and how many feet are needed to cross the room.

You may also supply the children with some exciting shapes to use for their measuring, including, for example, toy snakes or cardboard dragons. **Copymaster 23** (Exciting things to measure with) can be copied on to card and the shapes cut out and used for measuring.

Copymaster 24 (Measuring: non-standard units) gives the children opportunities to record their measuring.

Activity 2: Covering with books, cartons and blocks

Begin work on area by asking the children what they think area is. Play at estimating; for example, how many books will cover the carpet, how many cornflake cartons will cover a chair seat, and how many matchboxes will cover a word book. Let the children set their own tasks in finding 'how many... cover a...' Compile a class book for the reading corner.

Activity 3: Jugfuls and mugfuls

Structure the children's water play by setting them estimating and measuring tasks, using a variety of containers. When they are adept at the practical work, let them begin to record their findings and then set them problems.

Copymaster 25 (Capacity) poses some problems which the children can try to solve.

Activity 4: Weighing with Plasticine®, blocks and Multilink®

Assemble a weighing table complete with balls of Plasticine®, wooden blocks and Multilink®, and a tray of things to weigh. Set a number of practical tasks which the children can do in turn. They can then complete their own weighing tasks and picture record.

Activity 5: Who is quicker?

Try timing by counting. Ask a child to count while another child jumps up and down 20 times. Let the children invent their own 'timing' methods. They could include measuring tasks like these:

- Holding their breath
- Reading a page of a book aloud
- Recalling ten colours
- Doing a simple jigsaw.

As timing devices children could use chalk marks on a board, cuts in paper, drops into a box using a building block, or other things that the children can devise.

Try making sand clocks and water clocks and using these as timing devices. For example, the children could set each other tasks to do while one scoop of sand runs through the timer, or while the water clock drips ten droplets.

area book

It takes **8** books to cover the table

It takes **15** children to cover the carpet

Sand clock

scoop

sand box

cut down plastic bottle

dry sand

small hole

shoe box

pot or beaker

Water clock

bowl of water

measuring jug

cut down plastic bottle

water

tiny hole

pot or beaker

WHY WE AGREE ON MEASURES TO USE

Commentary
Only when children understand the need for standard measures can they begin to appreciate just how carefully measurement must be done; thus it is important to discuss standard measures.

Activity: Comparing results
Assemble some of the children's results from the previous activities under 'Starting to measure' and let the children look at them carefully. Record their discussion on tape, or write up the important points they make. They should be able to make connections, for example, between the size of their hands and the number of handspans each of them takes to measure a table. This is the point at which to begin to introduce standard measures.

COMMON STANDARD MEASURES

Commentary
When metric measures (particularly decimal currency) were introduced to Britain, many teachers began to teach small children metric units only. The pace of change was grossly over-estimated and we are still using feet and yards, square yards, pints, pounds and ounces. As these are in common use, children need to know about them and be able to use them.

The introduction of different kinds of measuring units to measure similar things requires careful planning and sensitivity. Explain a metric measure in a different session from an imperial one. Let the children carry metric or imperial measures through a piece of work. For example, if you show them a full bottle of milk, go on to discuss how many $\frac{1}{2}$ pint drinks you can get from it, and not how many drinks each of 200 ml.

Once the children have been introduced to standard measures, encourage them to make estimates before they try to measure and get an answer. It is important that they should have an idea of what a metre or pint or minute looks or feels like, so that they can predict the 'order' of their answer.

Activity 1: Standard measures of length, width and breadth
In separate sessions show the children metre sticks, school rulers, tapes and spring rules. Let them create a set of homemade resources for measuring, including cardboard metre strips and string or 'tape' measures a metre long. Important units to cover in these sessions include metres and yards. Also discuss miles and kilometres with the children.

Activity 2: Standard measures of volume
In separate sessions tell the children about pints and litres. Do some measuring of liquids, and then let the children use graduated measuring jugs and beakers, and milk bottles, as well as the collection of unmarked containers already available. Make sure they know what litres and pints are.

Activity 3: Standard measures of 'weight'
Show children a pair of kitchen scales and bathroom scales. Discuss pounds and kilograms.

Activity 4: Measuring time
The standard measures of time will be more familiar to the children than some other standard measures. However, the fact that they talk about bedtimes and being late for school does not mean that they have an understanding of time. To give them a sense of an hour, you could have a 'time check' day, where you begin by 'clocking the children in', discuss with them the total amount of time there is in the school day and what your plans are for their activities. Each hour (or half hour) have a time check, and tell the children how much of the school day has passed.

Tell the children about the vocabulary of time, and about 12- and 24-hour clocks.

You can play 'What is a minute?' by asking the children to close their eyes, put up a hand, and then take it down when they think a minute has passed. Introduce a minute into music and rhythm work. With a minute timer, pairs of children can set each other a range of challenges, including some of the following. How many times in a minute can you:

- write your name
- sing 'Jack and Jill'
- run round the hall
- hop across the carpet
- blink your eyes
- touch your toes . . .

A second is a good time interval for banging a drum, hopping or jumping, playing maraccas, tapping your foot, stamping, winking and doing a quick repertoire of actions like you find in some machines.

On Tuesday we had a time check day

* at **9 o'clock** we were doing Register

* at **10 o'clock** we were doing Maths and Art

* at **11 o'clock** we were in Assembly

* at **12 o'clock** we stopped for lunch

We spent **3 hours** in school on Tuesday morning

The story of our Tuesday morning

Maths — measures and sums | paper butterflies | out to play | Assembly — our prayer | some good writing

NUMBER PLAY AT LEVEL 2

Commentary

The arena for giving the children number 'problems' should be an active practical situation. For example, sums about pocket money are more fun when you have play money and piggy banks. 'Problems' sorted out in a practical way are more like maths in real life. Create role play situations in which the children can do work on estimation, number bonds to ten, counting and halves and quarters. The possible range of situations is endless. We have chosen a few, and extended the work begun at Level 1 in these settings.

Activity 1: Play house

Use and extend the house set up for Level 1 work. For example:

The play house is a **maths workshop**

Paula's group only today

● Hang a picture with numbers of things in it on the play house wall
● Put a number of teddies and a number of dolls in the house
● Set the table with a number of places, and a matching (or not quite matching) number of chairs
● Put pans on the 'cooker'
● Put play fruit in the bowl
● Put shopping in the shopping basket.

You can then confine the use of the play house to a group of children doing this number work through the day.

Then set problems, including things like:

● How many teddies are at home today? How many dolls? How many toys altogether?

34

- How many trees in the picture? How many flowers? How many trees and flowers?
- How many people are going to have lunch?
- If yellow Ted eats two apples from the bowl, how many fruits will be left?
- If the things in the shopping basket cost 2p each, how much was spent on shopping?

Activity 2: Play shop

Extending the shop ideas you used at Level 1, you can begin to give the things prices up to 10p and ask the children to take a shopping list and buy and total their items. They can also do quite complex puzzles. If you have a 'corner shop' or little supermarket, they can try things like:

- Is the pop more expensive than the juice?
- Which is the cheapest pack of biscuits?
- Are Crunchflakes cheaper than Crummos?
- What can you buy for 10p?

- How much do six eggs cost?
- What is the best teatime bargain in the shop?
- If you have 10p to spend, and use only 8p, how much change will there be?

Or create a shop with a theme. Here are some ideas:

- Seaside shop, carrying sand toys, flags, pretend rock, correctly named seashells, postcards
- Gloves, handbags, scarves and hats
- Garden centre, stocking trowels, dibbers, flower pots, pretend packets of seeds, gardening gloves and pot plants (which could be real or models)
- Fruit and vegetables
- Stationery, cards and gifts
- Jewelry, including homemade badges, beads, wristwatches and clocks
- Birthdays, including cards, serviettes, paper cups, party bags, party hats and pretend cakes
- Christmas, including decorations, things for a tree, tags and cards

Activity 3: Play hospital

The hospital can become a health clinic, and the 'doctor' can estimate, record and count how many patients she has seen in a week. You can supply some invented records for the children to add to. Or you could recruit a play dentist to count, for example:

- The number of teeth
- Wiggly teeth
- How many teeth the patients have lost.

Charts and wall posters can help. There are lots of measures and potential for health education here.

Activity 4: Play post office

At the post office, the children can learn about savings, licences, allowances, and buy little books of stamps. You can wrap parcels of predetermined weights and they can work out what the postage is. The post office can stock things of varying prices including pencils, rubbers and pens; party invitations, serviettes and paper cups; envelopes and writing paper.

Activity 5: Play telephone

Extend the work done in the play telephone box by pricing each call and asking the children to add up their calls. You can vary the price of calls by saying that calls to people inside the building are 10p and outside (just outside the building) are 20p. You can give a scale of prices for calls according to when they are made: attach a notice in the box to say that morning calls are 20p and afternoon calls half price.

It may be sensible to discuss with the children the real cost of phone calls!

It's easy to phone a friend!

price of calls:
in school   10p
outside   20p
far away   30p

It's **cheaper** to phone in the afternoon, ...it is **half price**

Activity 6: Play spaceship

List the planets in the solar system. Ask the children to decide where they are going and in what order. Make up ideas for space meals.

Travel in the Spaceship 'Stella'... ...which planets will you visit?

Solar System Tours

Mercury   Venus   Earth   Mars   Jupiter   Saturn   Uranus   Neptune   Pluto

Rocket fast food

meteorite pizza   Saturnburger   low-gravity juice   fizzling fries   deep-space do·nut   booster bar

REVIEW: NUMBER SO FAR ▶

By the end of Level 2 work, children should have the foundations laid for the numbers they will need and manipulate throughout their lives. It is at this point that we need to woo back the children who seem to have already decided that numbers are not for them, re-examine our own prejudices and detect whether we put children off by our manner or delivery and have a vision of the world of number, as the children have experienced it so far.

The important basics that we would see at this level are:

Exploration of number patterns
Further development of counting
Place value
Number bonds and addition and subtraction
Commutativity and associativity
Further development of problem-solving approaches
An understanding of our coinage
Early fraction work
Estimation
An understanding of the importance of standard measures.

Also by now, the children should have a growing understanding of the nature and importance of comparisons through encounters with:

- metres and kilometres
- yards and miles
- pints and litres
- kilograms and pounds
- hours and minutes.

We have stressed that as children start to move into written recording there is the danger that 'pages of sums' might come to be seen as the most significant indicator of mathematical work. While we understand the need for reinforcement and, at times, the security of doing something you can already do, we would add to this list of mathematical basics the need to avoid endless repetition.

Attainment Target 2: Number, Level 3

Pupils should understand and use number, including estimation and approximation, interpreting results and checking for reasonableness.

Programme of study

Pupils should engage in activities which involve:

- reading, writing and ordering numbers to at least 1000, and using the knowledge that the position of a digit indicates its value.
- learning and using addition and subtraction facts to 20 (including zero).

- learning and using multiplication facts up to 5 × 5 and all those in the 2, 5 and 10 multiplication tables.

- solving problems involving multiplication or division of whole numbers or money, using a calculator where necessary.
- understanding remainders in the context of calculation and knowing whether to round up or down.

- making estimates based on familiar units.
- recognising that the first digit is the most important in indicating the size of a number and approximating to the nearest 10 or 100.

- using decimal notation in recording money.
- recognising negative whole numbers in familiar contexts, e.g. a temperature scale, a number line, a calculator display.
- using a wider range of metric units of length, capacity, 'weight', and standard units of time.
- choosing and using appropriate units and instruments; interpreting numbers on a range of measuring instruments, with appropriate accuracy.

Statements of attainment

Pupils should be able to:

a) Read, write and order numbers up to 1000.

b) Demonstrate that they know and can use multiplication tables.

c) Solve problems involving multiplication or division.

d) Make estimates based on familiar units of measurement, checking results.

e) Interpret a range of numbers in the contexts of measurement or money.

Examples

Pupils could:

Use dice to generate three digits; make as many three-digit numbers as you can; read them out and order them.
Explain that four hundred and two is written 402 and why neither 42 nor 4002 is correct.

Give at least three possibilities for ○ and △, given ○ × △ = 20.
Explain that if tickets cost £4 each, only four can be bought with £18.

Find the cost of four calculators at £2.45 each.
Find out how many ways seating can be arranged for 25 children in rows of not more than 10. Which is the best way?

Estimate the height of a door in metres.
Estimate in centimetres the size of paper needed to design and make a greetings card.
Estimate the time it will take to clear away the PE equipment/art material

Read digital clocks correctly and analogue clocks to the nearest labelled division.
Read a thermometer, a stopwatch, a ruler, the dial on kitchen scales.
Appreciate that three £1 coins plus six 1p coins is written as £3.06 and that 3.6 on a calculator means £3.60 in the context of money.

NUMBERS TO 1000 AND PLACE VALUE

C26–8, R2, 3, 5

Commentary

At Level 2 the children will have worked on how we write numbers, and how the placing of a digit affects what we read. Revise this, using ones and tens (Cuisenaire® or Colour Factor®) or spent matches and elastic bands to make bundles of ten. Then try some more consolidation activities.

The children can make some 'big' numbers on a calculator to put into their books.

Activity 3: Patterns of ten

The children will, by now, be familiar with the pattern of tens up to 100. Let them count on in tens, and then make patterns with hundreds. They can fill in the

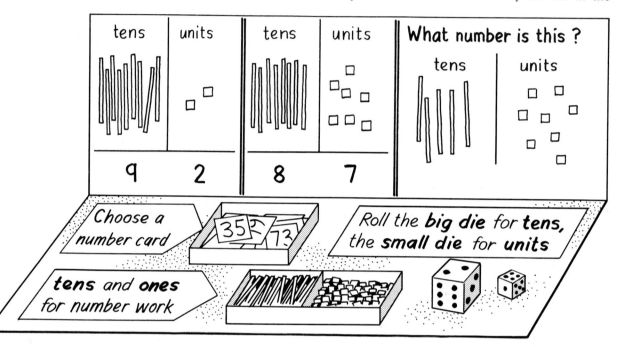

Activity 1: Tens and units 'columns'

Show the children how to draw columns in their books for 'tens' and 'units'. Using a class chart, record some numbers up to 100 on this. Then let the children put some into their books. They can throw two dice to assemble the digits.

There is a sheet of numbers to transfer to 'tens' and 'units' columns on **copymaster 26** (Tens and units).

Activity 2: Really big numbers

Now do similar work to that in Activity 1, using numbers in the hundreds and thousands.

Copymaster 27 (Thousands, hundreds, tens and units) presents a sheet of numbers to place in 'thousands', 'hundreds', 'tens' and 'units' columns.

numbers on a hundred square, and then lay these out to make 'hundreds' and a thousand.

Resource copymasters R2 and **R3** give hundred squares. **Resource copymaster R5** is a sheet of centimetre squares which can be used to cut out configurations of large numbers.

Activity 4: Numbers in words

When the children can tell by looking at a number whether it has 'hundreds' or 'tens' in it, give them some numbers written out as words, which they must convert to numerals.

Copymaster 28 (Big numbers in words) gives some examples that the children must translate.

ADDITION AND SUBTRACTION TO 20

C29, 30 R5

Commentary

The children should have mastered all the addition and subtraction facts to 10 at Level 2. Now they need to extend that knowledge to 20. Through rehearsal of computation, using counting aids, and recording their efforts, they should be able to commit important number bonds to memory. This is not rote learning, if they fully understand what is happening to the numbers.

Now is the time to establish 'zero' in the children's calculations. Activities relating to this concept and negative numbers are discussed in 'Zero and below' in this section.

In moving from number facts which should be memorised to the manipulation of 'sums' on paper, there is a tendency to teach children a standard method (algorithm) for doing those calculations. It is important to be circumspect about teaching such algorithms. There are a variety of standard algorithms and not one best method; children's own methods need exploration, and teaching children to 'crack a code' has to be matched with their understanding.

Activity 1: Patterns

The children can make patterns of number to 20 on small squared paper. There is a sheet of centimetre squares on **resource copymaster R5**.

The children can use Unifix®, Multilink®, Colour Factor® or other counting aids, and set out the pattern of bonds to 20. **Copymaster 29** (Subtraction bonds to 20) is a practice sheet.

Activity 2: Rehearsing and checking

Do not make children do pages and pages of 'sums', in the hope that number bonds to 20 will be absorbed. Try as many different ways of presenting them as you can think of, including, for example, the following:

● Check your answers on the calculator.
● Mark your friend's answers.
● Check your friend's answers on the calculator.
● List all the calculations that you can think of with the numbers 2 and 12 in them.
● Start with $10 + 2 = ?$. Underneath it write another calculation where only one of the figures is one more or one less than before. Do this again and again until you have done all you can.
● Create calculations with two ten-sided dice.

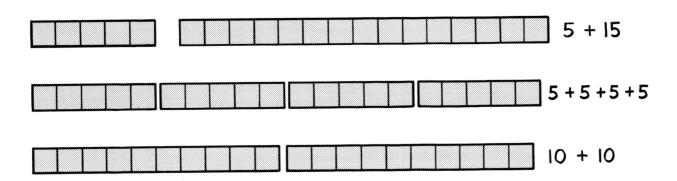

5 + 15

5 + 5 + 5 + 5

10 + 10

Activity 3: Oral addition and subtraction

Spend a couple of minutes each day in oral number work, so that, as quick as a flash, the children can eventually do the following:

● Compute in their heads, all the bonds to make exactly 20; for example, 6 and 14, 10 and 10.
● Compute in their heads all the subtraction facts to 20; for example, 20 minus 2 is 18.
● Know all about addition and subtraction within 20; for example, that $5 + 3 + 7 = 15$ and that 11 can be made up of a range of numbers including, for example, 4, 4 and 3.

Activity 4: Addition and subtraction games

Make up 'Bingo' and 'Snap' cards to play games using number bonds to 20.

A suitable game is given on **copymaster 30** (Bingo). You may like to ask the children to make their own, which they can play at home.

Photocopy copymaster 30 on to card, then cut out the four base cards. Cut out the numerals and put them in a box. Four players take a base card each. A 'caller' takes a numeral out of the box and calls it out. The first player to find an addition or subtraction on their base card to which the number is the answer is given the numeral, and covers the calculation. The winner is the first player to cover their base card.

▶ BEGINNING MULTIPLICATION

Commentary

Multiplication and division are generally regarded as being much more difficult operations for children to understand than addition and subtraction. The links that adults may see between, for example, multiplication and repeated addition, are not obvious to children and lots of varied work will be needed to forge such links.

Multiplication and division are inextricably linked. However, because we think it is easier to tackle one kind of work with numbers at a time, we have chosen to introduce them to the children separately. It is important to make links, when the children understand both operations.

It is a moot point as to whether the teaching of multiplication should precede the teaching of division. 'Sharing' is often more common in the previous experience of children. It is worth considering using some 'sharing' talk alongside your early work in multiplication.

Activity 1: Playing 'lots of'

This kind of play demands a special resource box which has a number of toys and other items displaying features to be included in 'lots of' counting. Include things like these:

model people (2s – legs and arms)
socks (2s – pairs)
mittens or gloves (2s – pairs)
2p coins (2s)
triangles (3s – sides and corners)
model milking stools (3s – legs)
three-bead necklaces (3s – beads)
model animals (4s – legs)

model cars (4s – wheels)
bunches of paper flowers (5s – flowers in each bunch)
5p coins (5s)
egg boxes (6s – eggs)
10p coins (10s).

Using such a resource bank the children will be able to grasp the concept of a 'lot'. Remind them that they can use their knowledge of number patterns to work out the total in a number of 'lots'.

The children can then set out repeated displays of 'lots of' using their own display cards, or ones that you have made for them.

Activity 2: Picture 'lots of'

Let the children record in their books, the results of some picture 'lots of' sums. This could include a 'mountain' of 3s or a tower of 5s.

It can be helpful for the children to recreate the number patterns in 'lots of' and put them into a little book, which they can keep. It is a 'tables' book in disguise! Class charts can be created too.

40

FIRST MULTIPLICATIONS

Commentary

Now that the children are beyond the stage of being starter mathematicians, they should be able to take the step from talking about 'lots of' to 'times' quite readily.

Again you should be wary of introducing a particular standard algorithm as *the* way to do multiplications. For many children the algorithm can assume more importance than the concept of multiplication.

Activity 1: Practical 'times' calculations

Using the resource bank from 'Beginning multiplication' Activity 1, the children can set out and talk you through their maths. Note that, from saying things like '3 lots of legs', you can encourage them to move towards saying things like '3 lots of 2'. They can match what they have done to an appropriate problem card, which also has all the counting information on it.

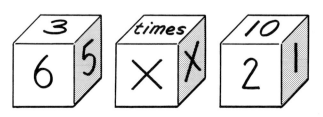

Activity 2: 'Times' language and sign

Use 'times', 'multiply' and the sign '×' with the children, and add them to the maths language book or chart in class.

Activity 3: Multiplications

These need to involve larger numbers for children to see the pattern in multiplication. Give them number patterns where they fill in what is missing. **Copymaster 31** (Missing numbers) is a sheet of such puzzles.

Use all your ingenuity to create and recreate multiplication bonds, using a variety of layouts and vocabulary and dice, including a blank one on which you can write the mathematical signs.

Activity 4: Multiplication using the calculator

As with addition and subtraction, calculators are invaluable for marking, checking and setting multiplications, and checking out patterns of number.

Activity 5: Oral multiplication

Practise tables! The tables mean nothing unless the children understand what they are doing with the numbers, but it is an asset to know, apparently without thinking, that 36 follows 27 in a pattern of 9s, for example. Try these:

● Start a pattern and see if the children can detect what the next but one number will be – 0, 3, 6, 9, ?, ? (answer 15)

● Give a 'middle' of the pattern and see if the children can 'count down' in the pattern as well as up – 26, 24, 22, 20, ? (answer 18, 16, 14, 12)

Activity 6: Multiplying games

The same sorts of games can be used for multiplying as for other operations. 'Bingo' and 'Snap' are applicable. Board games need to be ingenious to avoid the winner reaching the end in one mighty bound!

Copymasters 32 and **33** (Zap!) make a multiplication board game for two to four players. Photocopy copymaster 33 on to card, and cut out the multiplication cards. Place them face down in a pile. The players throw an ordinary die in turn, moving their counter as usual. If they land on a 'Zap' square, they turn over the top card and work out the multiplication, the other players checking the answer using a calculator. If the players' answer is wrong, they miss a turn.

Copymaster 34 (Multiplication ladders) is a game for four players, using two pentagonal spinners (**resource copymaster R1**), one marked 1 to 5, the other 6 to 10. Each player has a 'tables' ladder, cut from a copy of copymaster 34. In turn, they spin one spinner of their choice, and enter the answer to the multiplication on their card that starts with the number on the spinner. The winner is the first player to complete their ladder. (Answers should be checked with a calculator.)

41

BEGINNING DIVISION

Commentary

Even before they are formally introduced to division, the children will have a concept of what it means in real life. The challenge for you is to introduce the ways for recording what 'sharing' does to numbers, without divorcing it from the idea of sharing toys with their sisters and brothers or cheese sandwiches with their mum. No matter how competent children are as mathematicians, do not be tempted to leave out the practical work. Only links with real situations will convince many children that maths is relevant to them.

At Level 2, the children have met a half and a quarter. You may want to revise this work with them. The children will also have worked on multiplication. You will discover when it is appropriate to link multiplication and division. If the children have been given the confidence to play with numbers, some of them will find and point out the links themselves.

Activity 1: Playing 'sharing'

To play sharing, you and the children need access to a special resource box. Some of the things that might be found there are listed in Beginning multiplication, Activity 1, 'Playing "lots of"' above. Show the children that you can share play objects between a number of children or a number of toys. Avoid remainders at this stage.

Practise sharing out by, for example, sharing pencils between pencil cases, books into boxes and beads on to necklaces.

Let the children have many turns at sharing things out. Link their practical sharing to the moral dilemmas in sharing, and make up a little book of stories the children have written about what they share, at home and at school. Display the book in the maths or book corner, or use it as the basis for an assembly.

Activity 2: Picture 'sharing'

Let the children record in their books, the results of some picture 'sharing'. Set these out so that the children can join the shared item to the sharer.

Copymaster 35 (Picture sharing) presents some sample examples for the children to do.

FIRST DIVISIONS

Commentary

Children who understand addition, subtraction and multiplication, will quickly be able to convert their practical 'sharing' activity, using each other and toys, to an activity they can set out on a table or in their books. Now is the time to give them the mathematical words and sign for division. But, once again, be careful about setting the method as the challenge rather than the concept of division.

Activity 1: Practical 'share by'

Using practical resources, let the children set out and talk you or their friends through some 'share by' examples. Give them problem cards, with all the items for counting on them. The children can then lay out the counting aids to match each card, and use the resources to find the answer.

Activity 2: 'Share by' language and sign

Use 'shared between', 'division', 'divided by', 'size of share' and the sign '÷' with the children and add them to the maths language book or class chart.

Activity 3: Division

The children will need to record the patterns in these problems. Before you give them random problems, let them see what happens to the size of share as the number to be shared increases, and work out how many shares there can be, of a given size, in a big number.

Copymaster 36 presents some division puzzles. **Copymaster 37** presents divide cards for the game of 'Zap!' which is on **copymaster 32**.

Activity 4: Division and multiplication links

If the children do not see the links between division and multiplication, and remark on them, use things from the resource box to point out that, for example, $6 \div 2 = 3$ and $2 \times 3 = 6$.

Let the children convert some multiplications to divisions.

Activity 5: Division using the calculator

Let children mark, check and set divisions using calculators. Now is the time to give them questions involving all four operations, allowing them to check their answers on the calculator.

Copymaster 38 (Calculator checks) is a mixed bag of calculations suitable for checking with a calculator.

Activity 6: Remainders

Show the children that if you share 9 sweets between Dawn and Jenny they will have 4 each and there will be 1 left over. Tell the children that this is called the 'remainder'. Play practical sharing with remainders.

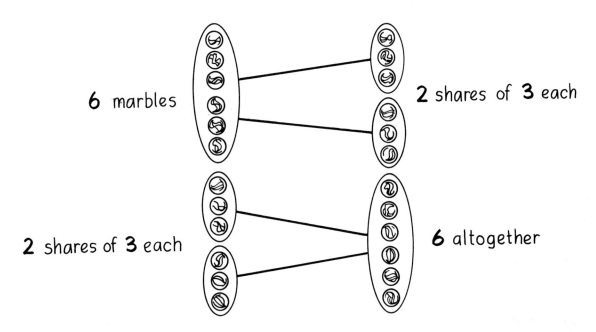

6 marbles — 2 shares of 3 each

2 shares of 3 each — 6 altogether

ESTIMATING MEASUREMENTS

Commentary

Estimation is an integral part of the mastery of measurement. Without the ability to estimate, the children will not be able to solve measuring problems or cope with measures in life. It is therefore very important to let the children make estimates as often as is feasible.

Estimation in measurement, as in most mathematical work with children, is difficult to teach. One reason for this is the emphasis that we place in mathematics teaching on accuracy. From the child's viewpoint, on the one hand we are asking for the production of the one right answer but on the other we ask for a set of best guesses. It is important, therefore, to help children to see estimation as an integral part of the process at arriving at solutions which are good enough in the given circumstances. For example, while we need to estimate the whole number of rolls of wallpaper we need for decorating (and we know that some will be

left over), we need a more precise solution to cutting a length of wood to make a shelf.

Activity: Estimating measurements

As soon as the children have been introduced to a measure, they can start to use it in their estimations. When you set them problems, ask them to make an estimate before they measure. Give them oral problems to solve. For example:

● Could a giant a metre wide get through the classroom door?
● How much water do the fish need in the aquarium if they are used to a minimum depth of 20 cm?
● How does the 'weight' of 10 pencils compare with that of 10 crayons?
● How many times can you count in twos to 20 in a minute?

There are endless possibilities.

APPROXIMATION ▶

Commentary
In adult life approximation is a skill we use a great deal. If there is £9.87 in our purse, we know that we have nearer ten pounds than nine. A half-full bag of flour, marked 1 kilogram, will contain approximately a pound of flour. Approximations make it easier to solve number problems. If we are buying a fence for the perimeter of the garden we know that 106.531 46 metres is not the level of accuracy needed in working out how many fencing panels to buy. Approximations and estimations are not the same; we use the former to determine the latter.

Activity 1: Give an approximation
Give the children the solutions to some problems and results of some experiments, and ask for an approximation of these.

Activity 2: Effects of approximation
Discuss with the children, the dilemmas we all face when we find something out and want to tell other people of our findings. This applies in all kinds of research situations. For example:

● Mum has discovered how many biscuits the family eats in a fortnight.
● Survey researchers have established how often Britons say they take a bath.

Should mum say, 'The family have eaten 96 biscuits in two weeks,' or 'Six packets of biscuits have gone in a fortnight!'? Which will make more impact on the family? Which is more accurate? Which is more useful for mum to know, if she is going to buy less in future? It may be that the approximation, that is the number of packets, is the more potent information.

So, too, would be the revelation that approximately one in ten Britons have a bath once a month!

Use some of the results the children have obtained in their research to work out approximations and their implications.

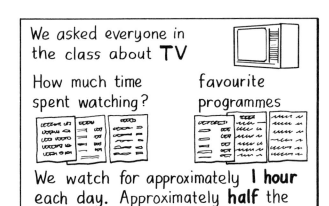

We asked everyone in the class about TV

How much time spent watching?

favourite programmes

We watch for approximately **1 hour** each day. Approximately **half** the class like cartoons best.

RECORDING MONEY ▶

C39 –42

Commentary
The children will have played with replica coins at Level 2. They should have had a chance to have a close look at real coins and notes and discuss equivalence. Now is the moment to introduce the decimal point.

While the use of a decimal point is at the heart of how we record money it is important to remember that conventions in money work do not follow, in some important respects, the conventions in decimal work. For example, we do not write £1.40 as £1.4 – we always show whole numbers of pence after the decimal point.

Activity 1: Using pounds and pence
Use play coins, and print some play £5 and £10 notes. With the children, look at the values of these, match equivalent values in different coinage and discuss how we write this down on a bill. Show the children some real bills, including, for example, an electricity bill, a supermarket checkout slip and a bill from the garage or window cleaner. Use these as a basis for a display.

Tell the children about the decimal point in money, that that is what it is called, and that it marks where the number of pence begins. Make sure they understand that we have to be careful to write 08 after a decimal point, if we mean 8p, because there is a 'tens' column there.

Copymaster 39 (Tickets, bills and receipts) presents a number of bills, receipts and price layouts for discussion, and a shopping list and bill for the child to complete.

Activity 2: Writing pounds and pence
Create a shop window display. It need not have real things in it. Pin price tags to each item, and then set the children a number of tasks requiring them to make out bills and work out change.

The children can also convert prices to decimal notation and back again. They will need plenty of practice in doing this.

There are some money problems on **copymaster 40**.

Copymasters 41 (Shopping – track) and **42** (Shopping lists) make a board game. Photocopy on to card copymaster 42 and cut out these 'shopping lists'. Give one list and £3.50 in play money to each of three players. Let a fourth child be 'banker/shopkeeper' with a box of change and a calculator to check the players' spending. The winner is the first to buy all the items on their list (thereby spending all their money).

ZERO AND BELOW

Commentary

The concept of zero is familiar to children when they are very young. 'All gone' is in the vocabulary of most toddlers. Negative numbers are much more difficult to understand. One of the few ways we meet them in everyday life is in measuring temperature, and we have taken it as our example here.

One of the values in using a number line with children in their early number work is that its use can be extended below zero by counting backwards from a whole number.

Activity 1: Counting using zero

Use zero in all the oral counting you do with the children. For example, start their counts in 10s with zero, and their counts of children and experimental results. Add zero to all the number resources and charts available to the children.

Activity 2: Computation using zero

Use 0 in calculations you give to the children. Do not let their answers go below zero. Try to present as many different configurations of numbers as possible, giving the children work in addition and subtraction, and including a variety of layouts, for example:

$$5 + 0 = ? \qquad 0 + 12 = ?$$

$$17 +$$
$$0$$
$$\overline{}$$

$$16 - 0 = ? \qquad 4 - ? = 0$$

Activity 3: Calculators and zero

Point out that calculators always start you off at zero. Let the children use them to do, check and create calculations.

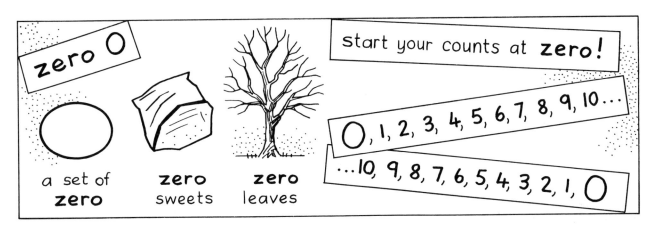

a set of **zero**

zero sweets

zero leaves

start your counts at **zero!**

0, 1, 2, 3, 4, 5, 6, 7, 8, 9, 10...

...10, 9, 8, 7, 6, 5, 4, 3, 2, 1, 0

Activity 4: Looking at negative numbers

Show the children a freezer thermometer, and let them draw a picture of it, showing the scale. If possible, examine the thermometer while it is in a freezer and has a negative reading. Show the children a maximum and minimum thermometer. Let them draw and record the scale on that. If you can, record a night temperature of less than zero, so that they can see the thermometer in operation.

Let the children do an investigation into climate, to find out all they can. Their findings might include, for example:

● those areas of the world where the temperature is often below zero
● where people live at temperatures below zero
● the temperature of the coldest place on earth.

Make a *Negative Number Facts* book to add to a display or the book corner.

Activity 5: Making negative numbers

Show the children what happens when you subtract, for example, 7 from 5 using a calculator. Let the children create calculations involving negative numbers and record them in their books.

negative numbers

living below zero

Copymaster 43 is a sheet of examples which can be done with or without a calculator, where some of the answers are negative numbers.

45

STANDARD MEASURES

Commentary

At Level 2 the children were introduced to common imperial and metric measures. They can now begin to work with the other metric units in general use, like the gram and centimetre.

Now that the children will attempt measurement in small units, it is even more important to stress the need for carefulness.

Activity 1: A centimetre rule

Show the children that a metre can be cut into 100 equal pieces, each piece being called a centimetre. Give the children card strips a metre long with centimetre divisions, and let them mark on the numerals. They can use this strip to measure around the classroom and school.

Copymaster 44 (Measuring in centimetres) gives some practice.

When the children are proficient at measuring they can apply this skill in other areas of the curriculum

Activity 3: Weighing in kilograms and grams

Sugar is commonly sold in kilogram bags, so a full bag would give children an idea of how a kilogram feels. They can then estimate how much they themselves weigh and test their estimates on some bathroom scales. Help the children to tabulate their results.

Pack in sealed transparent plastic bags 1 gram, 2 grams, 3 grams, 5 grams and 10 grams of some common foodstuffs. You could include, for example, uncooked pasta, semolina, dessicated coconut, raw oats, loose tea, spice, herbs, dried beans, rice and barley. Arrange these in a display so that the children can freely handle them and compare them.

Let the children use a classroom balance to weigh some things from the mathematics resource box. Pre-select some items to ensure a range of experience. Let the children compare the results they obtain. They

Guess your weight!	our estimates		what we weighed
A bag of sugar weighs **1 kilogram**	Pat	20 kg	21 kg
Suzanne weighs the same as **20 bags** of sugar	Howard	22 kg	22 kg
	Leo	25 kg	24 kg
	Bethan	23 kg	21 kg

well done, Howard!

including technology and art. For example, they can measure some material and make glove puppets.

Activity 2: Litres and millilitres

We buy fruit juice in litres, and milk is sold in supermarkets in litres. Examine some packaging and containers with the children to see what is measured in litres. Let the children do cooking and use metric measures.

Copymaster 45 (Litres and millilitres) gives practice in measuring millilitres.

should all agree – discuss the possible reasons for any discrepancies. Depending on the construction of the balance, discuss with the children the kinds of things that can be weighed easily on it and its optimum range in terms of 'weight'. If you can, let the children look closely at other kinds of weighing machine, like a letter scales, a spring balance, and those the school nurse uses, and discuss their likely ranges.

Use an accurate kitchen balance in cooking, and let the children do the weighing.

Look at and compare these little bags of food

| 10g rice | 5g coconut | 20g beans | 2g tea | 50g barley | 30g pasta | 2g spice |

| 1g herbs | 5g tea | 3g oats | 20g pasta | 10g coffee | 20g sugar | 5g rice |

Activity 4: Telling the time

Children do need to be told exactly what happens to the hands on a clock, and how to tell the time from it. An enormous clock face, with every minute marked, the quarters and half past, and arabic numerals for the numbers helps. There is a small clock face on **copymaster 46** to which the children can add hands.

Make a game of reading the clock face. Use a play clock and do oral work to enable children to learn from one another. Here are some of the written presentations which you can use to give the children plenty of practice with conventional clocks.

● Clock face with time written in – child puts in hands

● Clock face with hands – child writes the time
● Two clock faces with hands – child works out time difference
● Clock face with long hand missing – child writes in time.

Tie in work on the hour with the children's daily routine. The quarter and half hours may sometimes tally with playtimes and assembly times. Collect these significant times and display them.

Set challenges like 'In an hour's time what will the clock say?' 'The minute hand has fallen off this clock. Can we still use it to tell the time?'

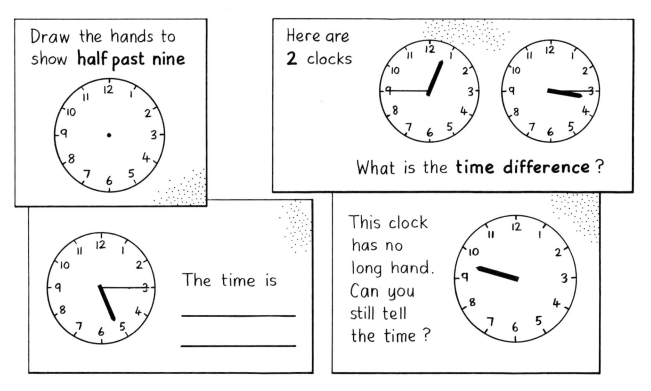

Draw the hands to show **half past nine**

Here are **2 clocks**

What is the **time difference**?

The time is

_____

_____

This clock has no long hand. Can you still tell the time?

Copymaster 47 (Telling the time) includes some time puzzles.

Look at digital times too. A cardboard number rest with a box of small cards with numerals on them and a card with a point or two points on it can be used to set up times.

Make a display where the children can come and set the hands on a clock, change the digital time, match the clock to the classroom clock, and put on the clock lunchtime, playtime, lighting-up time, high tide, the time of the next train to the city and other times important in your community.

Copymasters 48 (Digital/written time) and **49** (Time) give the children opportunities for some practice work on time.

CHOOSING AND USING INSTRUMENTS

Commentary

If the children have had a wide range of practical experiences in measuring, they themselves will now be able to decide which instrument to use for which measuring job.

Once the children start to use standard measures, all their measuring work is 'action' based and like 'real life'. We have therefore not attempted to set up role play situations but suggest instead a series of projects which will take the children into an investigation of real measures.

Try to alert the children to all the incidental learning opportunities, by, for example, looking at the sizing on Dana's new coat and discussing how and where it is measured, and what size shoes most children have.

Activity 1: How to measure investigations
Set some open-ended investigations which children can do alone and in twos. Here are some possibilities:

a) Pretend you are building a new hutch for a rabbit, or cage for a budgie. Decide on the materials, the approximate size, the tools you would need (including measuring tools), the units you would do your measuring in and what you would need to know about the rabbit. List all these things, and do a sketch of how the hutch will look.

b) You are the designer of a bench seat for two children to sit on. What measuring tools do you need, and what do you need to know about the children?

c) Find out how long it takes for everyone to come in from the playground, after the whistle has blown. What did you use to do your measurements? Could you have measured it in some other way?

d) A good way to make pastry is to add to the bowl half as much fat as you have flour. Make some pastry using 80 grams of fat. How much flour do you need? Rub the mixture until it looks like fine breadcrumbs, and then add a tiny amount of water, so that you can make a dough. Roll it out $\frac{1}{2}$ cm thick and cut into 8 cm circles. Put in a patty pan, add a little jam to each. Ask an adult to put them in a hot oven for 10 minutes. How many tarts did you make? What would you need to make twice as many?

e) What is the difference in 'weight' between the lightest and the heaviest person in the class? What did you use to make the measurements? (Be careful of children's sensitivities if you set this project.)

Activity 2: Projects using measures
a) Interview a school architect about some of the things they take into account when designing a school. Discuss with them the children's ideas about how their current school design could be changed to better accommodate children of primary age. For example, the children could ask for window sills not to stick out at eye level, display boards not to be $1\frac{1}{2}$ metres off the ground, and corridors to the playground to be wider.

Our designs for an ideal school

Jennifer — **big windows**

Lee — **soft play areas**

Sadaf — **tall buildings, fast lifts**

David — **beautiful gardens**

b) Discuss with the children the optimum size for a desk, working surface, or exercise book. They will have opinions about working in too small a space or on paper that gets scuffed at the corners. They could make their own books to match their ideals. Discuss the dimensions of pens, pencils and crayons for ease of handling and working. For example, manufacturers produce 'fat' crayons and thick brushes for small hands. Do the children themselves find these easier to work with?

How we like to work

the best size of:

book

pencil

brush thin

paper

table

c) Do a classroom temperature check (the children may not be ready to read the thermometer themselves (see Science AT 3 Level 4) so you can read it and band the recordings cold ... cool ... warm ... too warm). Ask a sample of children how they find the temperature.

Ask those same children to report on how they felt when they first went outside to play. Discuss and display the results.

d) Ask the school doctor or nurse to talk to the children about our fluid needs. They can say what a baby needs, what we need every day, and which drinks are healthy.

e) Ask the officials at the local swimming pool to give you some details about the dimensions of the pools, how much water they hold, how often they are cleaned and what is added to the water.

f) If there is a reservoir near the school, ask the officials there for the statistics about it. How much does it hold? How much water does it take for it to rise 1 cm? How many people get their water from it? How much water does a family use in a day?

g) Let the children prepare food and drinks and do cooking to produce healthy food, and have practice in measuring out liquids and weighing ingredients.

h) Visit a post office and look at the letter scales and parcel scales. Look at the cost of sending letters and parcels of different weights.

i) Make a variety of clocks, using sand, water, candles (close supervision required) and make sundials with the children (see Science AT 4 Level 3). Examine the inside of a conventional wind-up clock to see how it works. Ask a local watch-mender or clock enthusiast to tell the children the main components of a clock (this will help their understanding of gears and levers). Look at railway and bus timetables and discuss the use of the 24-hour clock.

j) Investigate the use of timers in sport. Look at world records. Look at speedometers and trip meters on bicycles and in cars and discuss how we read them. Investigate speed limits.

Any of the above investigations could form the starting points for a topic, work for a display, open evening or assembly.

PLAY AT LEVEL 3

Commentary

Some teachers seem to feel that active play with number is the prerogative of the reception class. Our view is that, in all areas of learning, we are too quick to move away from real situations and first-hand experience to the abstract and information at second hand. We are not suggesting that 'exploratory' role play should be continued (except for the children who need it) beyond the first few terms of schooling. However, 'number play' situations continue to be appropriate throughout all the classes in the primary school. At Level 3, you will see that we have extended what is expected in those same play situations that we worked on at Level 2. We have focused the situations a little more. The tasks set are carefully specified, and the 'play' situation need only be set up for the time it takes for the appropriate children to do the work. If your working space, ingenuity and time permit, it would be possible to create, for example, a play post office, where all the children have a go at doing the tasks appropriate for each of them, whether they are working at Level 1, 2 or 3.

Activity 1: Play house

Give the children a series of problems to do, using the play house as their starting point. For example:

● Give the house a number, and ask the children which house numbers would appear on either side (odds and evens).
● Create an inventory of contents, and ask the children to check it out, including things like: 'How many items are in the cupboard? or 'How much money is in the purse?' (numbers to 20 and beyond).

● Create a calendar for the house, including birthdays and social events for the toys (computation and time).
● Make a play TV from a box and make up a *TV Times* of children's programmes (programme length and viewing hours).
● Write a menu for play house meals (counting, weighing, recipes, cooking times and temperatures, sequencing, health education).
● Write a shopping list to link with the menu (money, estimation, approximation).
● Start a database using the play house as the prototype, and include how many rooms, doors, windows and similar information. The children can collect the same information for their own or their classmates' homes, to add to the database.

Activity 2: Play shop

Set up a supermarket or theme shop, like those listed in 'Play shop' (page 35) at Level 2.

You could even set up a shop to serve both maths and English. One example is a 'story' shop, which is really a bank of resources that the children can use for story writing. The appeal is that it is flexible, for you can change the 'stock' and the children can choose what they 'buy' for their story. For example, with a spending limit of £1, or four items, Roxanne assembled for her story the following things:

model castle	60p
paper flag	2p
princess doll	30p
cardboard bridge	8p

She could begin her story with the tale of her 'magic' shopping trip, or the shopping could be part of maths and the story begins 'Once upon a time . . .'

On another day Asif might collect from the shop the following:

a 'giant' sock and a little one	total 50p
a large model cake	15p
a bag labelled 'magic dust'	32p

What a book of stories a group of children can produce! And each will be different.

Challenge the children when they are 'shopping' by asking them to create shopping lists, work out change, look for 'bargains' and take advantage of sales and special offers. If, for example, the children complete a shopping expedition one day, and the following day everything is half price, they can see what happens to the shopping bill.

Activity 3: Play post office

Extend the children's experience at Levels 1 and 2 by, for example, doing some of the following activities:

● Introduce the children to the course a real letter takes when it is posted, and role play the journey of a letter

● Look at the actual postal rates for letters and parcels, and create some letters and packets that can be weighed and the postage determined

● Make a study of addresses and postcodes, looking at patterns of numbering and what postcodes mean.

Activity 4: Play telephone

Extension activities, beyond the experience gained at Levels 1 and 2, could include the following:

● Play remembering number sequences and help the children to memorise their home telephone numbers

● Make the calls have a purpose now, and play 'fax' with messages they have typed on a typewriter or word processor

● Use the telephone book to set problem numbers to look up.

Activity 5: Play hospital

Real weighing and measuring can be introduced into the 'health clinic' at this level. The children can use height measures, scales and foot measures to determine and compare data about each other, for example:

Height in cm
Weight in kilograms and grams
Foot size.

Data can be used to make comparisons, draw graphs and test hypotheses. For example:

● Do the tallest people in the class have the biggest feet?

● Is the average height for the boys taller than for the girls?

● Do the girls' foot sizes have a bigger range than the boys?

Ideas about temperature and pulse rate can be introduced.

Activity 6: Play spaceship

Some more challenging activities here include:

● Let the children find out all they can about a recent space probe and record the numerical data.

● Draw their own race or maze game, using numbers and space as a theme.

● Find out earth information about time across the world.

51

REVIEW: NUMBER SO FAR

You can give yourself a tick for number if all the children whom you believe to have mastered Level 3 have:

● carried out a broad range of the kinds of activities we have presented so far
● fully understood one step before tackling the next
● gained an appreciation that you can play with numbers and find patterns
● not forgotten that numbers are important in everyday life.

The important basics that we would see at this Level are:

● Developing further understanding of place value
● An understanding of money
● Development of addition and subtraction
● The meaning of zero
● The foundations of multiplication and division
● Approximation and estimation.

In our opinion, there is much conceptual work to be done at Level 3. The speed of the children's progress through Levels 1 and 2 will depend to some extent on their experience of real numbers outside school. Though this does continue at Level 3, the expectation is that the children will be able to work with numbers in the abstract, outside their own experience. Some seven-year-olds may have seen 1000 of something, but it is hard to visualise, even as an adult. The key to Level 3 is to keep the numbers real as far as possible. It is also important to be careful in the imposition of any standard algorithms. There is now plenty of evidence to suggest that given, rather than home-grown, algorithms can dominate children's approaches and they can come to mask the mathematics!

In addition the children have now encountered almost all of the measures that they will need to be able to understand measuring and measurement when they are adults. This is not to say that they do not need more practice, particularly in making sensible choices of appropriate measures and measuring instruments, and in relating estimation to degrees of accuracy. In order to progress further, though, it is important that children master all of the major elements at this level. The basics are:

● familiarity with a range of imperial and metric measures
● telling the time using analogue and digital clocks
● selecting appropriate measures and not mixing measures
● an increasing understanding of how accurate you need to be in a given situation.

All of these need to be learned through practical investigation, and the practical nature of measurement work cannot be over-emphasised.

Attainment Target 3: Algebra

Pupils should recognise and use symbolic and graphical representation to express relationships.

For some people, *algebra* conjures up experiences of learning tricks that can be done with numbers and letters, but to no obvious purpose. It is an area of mathematics that provokes strong feelings. This is a pity because the purpose of algebra is to simplify understanding through the generation of generalisations about such things as number patterns or the path of a line on a graph. In tackling early work in algebra, we need to keep in mind the idea about generalising from the particular. For children to make sense of the purpose of algebra, they need the opportunity to work with lots of numbers before they can see a generalisable pattern.

There are two main ways in which the foundations of some aspects of algebra are found in primary classrooms. Children often encounter 'sums' which invite them to state what is the missing number. These are often of the form $4 + ? = 6$. While there are connections with algebraic ideas it must not be assumed that algebra is only about handling equations (although that is a skill within algebra), but rather that equations are formulations of general statements derived from sets of real data. It is important to understand what equations and formulae actually represent. The other encounter many children have is oral. It is when teachers ask for a general statement of the kind: 'What sort of a number (or sequence of numbers) is that?'

The foundations of algebra, as set out in the National Curriculum, pay attention in the early years to relationships and sequences as well as patterns and the generation of generalisations.

Resourcing algebra
The resource bank that we mention at the front of the book is appropriate for work in this section. Additional resources that may help include:

- A tape or record of sound patterns like birdsong and roadworks
- A camera and film
- Musical instruments
- Poetry books
- Feely bags
- An ark and animals
- A Celsius thermometer scale.

You may wish to pursue pattern-making ideas in art and technology. These will demand a variety of materials and media, including all those mentioned in the general resource bank.

Good use can be made of the newer technologies. Computers, good software and, if possible, 'robot' devices will reap rewards in both understanding and motivation.

Attainment Target 3: Algebra, Level 1

Pupils should recognise and use symbolic and graphical representation to express relationships.

Programme of study	Statements of attainment	Examples
Pupils should engage in activities which involve:	Pupils should be able to:	Pupils could:
• copying, continuing and devising repeating patterns represented by objects/apparatus or single-digit numbers.	a) Devise repeating patterns.	*Devise patterns such as:* *a potato print pattern: red, red, blue, red, red, blue, ...; a number pattern: 2, 1, 2, 1, 2, 1, 2, 1, ...; a shape pattern:* □, △, ○, □, △, ○, ...

PATTERNS AROUND US

Commentary
The beginnings of algebra, like all other branches of mathematics, should start in the real world, and with the children themselves.

Activity 1: The children themselves
Let the children create repeat patterns using themselves and their classmates, lining up for all to see. Here are some examples:

- boy/girl/boy/girl/ . . .

- with/without cardigans, long socks, white shirt or blouse, . . .
- caterpillar patterns, like one arm/one leg/one arm/ . . .

Let them try more sophisticated patterns, for example:

- two people with fair hair/two with dark hair/ . . .
- three five-year-olds/one six-year-old/ . . .
- one fan of 'Tom and Jerry'/one of 'Roadrunner'/ one of 'Mickey Mouse'/ . . .
- two people standing with arms up/one with arms down/ . . .

Activity 2: Everyday patterns
Encourage the children to look around the school and the immediate environment for patterns, both natural and designed. They may find things like patterns in brickwork and wallpaper, window sizes, plants in a garden border, railings, curtain designs, and floor tiles. In the natural world there are leaf attachment patterns, spots on ladybirds, ripples in a stream, branches on trees and flowers in blossom clusters. A range of patterns would make an impressive display, and could lead the children into other activities.

Activity 3: Pattern and human routines
Ask the children about the patterns in what they do every day. For example, 'wake up/get up/get dressed/ have breakfast/wash and clean teeth' may be one such routine. Look at routines in school, like 'register/ assembly/quiet reading/the order of work tasks/ play'. Discuss the patterns of meals in a day, hours in the day, days in a week, and other patterns that affect our everyday lives. Concertina books can be used to show a sequence, and children can be invited to say how their own routines vary from some examples.

Activity 4: Listening to patterns
The children can try describing or replicating patterns they hear. You can play recorded birdsong, sing songs with choruses, and listen to traffic noise and sounds of workmen digging up the road.

CREATING PATTERNS

Commentary
Pattern-making may not come after pattern investigation in children's intellectual development, for the noises and movements babies make and repeat may be early pattern-making rather than responses to the information their senses are giving them about the world. However, when the children have had plenty of opportunities to look at and for patterns, and to listen to patterns, they may be more adept at spotting pattern and creating more complex patterns themselves.

Arrange pattern-making activities so that they are as open-ended as possible, for, if a pre-set format is not imposed, there will be more variety in children's responses and greater learning opportunity available from the work of others.

When the children are asked to record pattern, in artwork or writing, they need to use techniques that get the pattern working quickly. For example, colouring in a repeat pattern of five red, then five yellow, then five blue beads, and repeating it again and again, may well outlast the enthusiasm of some children. If they can, say, print with red, yellow and blue potato cuts, the repeats will be done before the job becomes tedious.

When the children are skilful pattern-makers, look at the possibilities in 'orchestrating' their patterns. For example, how you display a set of painted patterns may demonstrate a rhythm which the children can tap out with sticks or shakers. A pattern of beads can translate into print on fabric. (See Activity 6, 'Pattern translation', on page 57.)

Activity 1: Human movement
During PE and dance sessions let the children work on movement sequences which have pattern. For example, to a tap on the tambour, the children can make a series of shapes in a sequence, returning to the start of the sequence when there are two quick taps.

'Machines' and 'Robots' are popular themes to explore, where movement routines can be repetitive and fun.

When the children have some movement routines developed, try getting them to work in pairs, first alongside one another, and then in pairs together. Keep the routines short, and let them watch each other's efforts and determine the patterns. If you want a record of the children's work, a set of photographs or tape of the children describing what they do would be a valuable addition to a display.

Activity 2: Making music
Make a music corner where the children can experiment with rhythm and sound patterns. Supply paper and pencil there too, so that they can experiment with ways to write down their patterns of 'music'.

When the children are gathered together and have a couple of minutes 'waiting time', try some clapping patterns, which they can copy.

Sing songs together, with repeats in the tune and in the words.

55

Activity 3: Patterns in words

Read poems which have a clear metre to the children. Let the children look for pairs of rhyming words and make up little rhymes to say. Sing the rhymes as a chant and try them as a round. Collect rhymes with rhythm for a class book.

Activity 4: Pattern in construction

Ask the children to create patterns with construction toys, including Lego®, wooden bricks, plastic straws, Duplo®, coloured Plasticine® and spent matches.

Activity 5: Pattern in artwork

Here are a few of the many possibilities. Colour, paint and draw blobs, triangles, beads on necklaces, buttons on jackets, stripes on snakes, rungs on ladders, stripes on trousers and tigers; print with hands, fingers and feet, boxes and other junk, potatoes and string, to make friezes, borders, book covers, drapes, and wrapping paper; made collages with repeat shapes in paper, card, cellophane, fabric, wool; construct paper chains, mobiles and towers from art materials.

Activity 6: Pattern translation
Try getting the children to use a pattern format in several ways. For example, they might invent a pattern with bricks, tap out that pattern on the drum, paint the pattern in stripes, and sign the pattern with coloured strokes on a piece of paper. Arrange a tempting display where the children can 'translate' each other's patterns into other modes of presentation.

Activity 7: Patterns of numerals
The children will be familiar with counting rhymes and numbers in sequence in their work on AT 2 Number. Let them record a pattern they can see, using numerals.

Next ask the children to create patterns using numerals, then to use these in their music or artwork.

PLAYING WITH PATTERNS

C50, 51

Commentary

There are many ways of increasing children's awareness of and sensitivity to pattern. We have listed some here. They could be seen as extension activities.

Until now we have not set children patterns to copy, continue or complete. This is because over-prescription can stifle creativity. If the children have had plenty of practice in the previous activities, then they can sometimes now be given a pattern to replicate.

Activity 1: A pattern-crazy day

Designate a day as, for example, a 1 2 1 2 day, and ask the children to try to bring the pattern into their tasks for the day (without going to extremes!). For example, they can pin a note on the door, saying 'Please give a KNOCK knock knock KNOCK knock knock'. Their maths can be related to numbers and shapes in these patterns. Their music-making can match the pattern. Their artwork can be based on this too. In dance or PE they can invent a march or a gymnastics routine based on the same 1 2 1 2 pattern. Home corner play can use the pattern; in serving up play dinner, the cook can give out one potato, two potatoes, and so on. At the end of the day, you should have a wealth of material for a display or an assembly – and all from one simple repeat pattern.

Activity 2: A pattern quiz

Give the children a set of patterns to look for. You can confine them to the classroom, or the school block, or you can let them take the quizzes home.

An example quiz is set out on **copymaster 50** (Patterns around you).

Activity 3: Repeat and try out

Try out some 'What comes next?' and 'What is after that?' patterns with the children.

Try setting up a pattern which the children have to continue and then test out. For example, a 3 1 2 4 pattern might be laid out in blocks or signed as dots on paper. The children can continue it and play the pattern on a percussion instrument or clap the pattern to see if it is correct.

Copymaster 51 (Number patterns) is a sheet of patterns to continue and check.

REVIEW: ALGEBRA SO FAR

The essence of mathematics lies in pattern, in creating, modifying, extending and explaining patterns of numbers, shapes, and ultimately ideas. Algebra is about pattern – it is like learning the rules of a game. The 'game' is mathematics, and the rules about pattern-making are embodied in algebra. These are strong arguments against the ideas that the children are wasting time when they are pattern-making, or that maths is only about doing sums!

The emphasis at Level 1 has been on raising the children's awareness of pattern. They should now know the following:

● There are patterns all around us
● Some patterns occur naturally, while others are designed
● We sometimes have a pattern or order of doing things
● We use numbers to talk about patterns
● We can sign a pattern using numerals.

The basic idea throughout this level is that of the identification of pattern.

Attainment Target 3: Algebra, Level 2

Pupils should recognise and use symbolic and graphical representation to express relationships.

Programme of study	Statements of attainment	Examples
Pupils should engage in activities which involve:	Pupils should be able to:	Pupils could:
• exploring and using patterns in addition and subtraction facts to 10. • distinguishing odd and even numbers.	a) Explore number patterns.	*Use counters to make various combinations to given totals.* $5 + 0 = 5 \quad 5 = 4 + 1$ $4 + 1 = 5 \quad = 3 + 2$ $3 + 2 = 5 \quad = 3 + 1 + 1$ $ = 2 + 2 + 1$ *etc.* $8 - 4 = 4$ $8 - 3 = 5$ *etc.*
• understanding the use of a symbol to stand for an unknown number.	b) Recognise the use of a symbol to stand for an unknown number.	*Find the missing numbers:* $3 + \blacksquare = 10$ $\bullet + 3 = 8$ $2, 4, 6, \square, 10$ *Suggest numbers that might fit into:* $\blacklozenge + \blacklozenge = \blacksquare$

PATTERNS IN ADDITION/SUBTRACTION TO 10

Commentary
The children should do this work in conjunction with their work on number. In fact, if they have had much practice in pattern-making, they will *expect* there to be a pattern in their number work.

In looking at number–algebra links, there are two important considerations. In tackling any mathematics activity it is vital not to see it in isolation from other areas of the curriculum, or from other areas of mathematics. Only through making explicit the links and interdependence between mathematical topics will we help the children to become numerate.

Activity 1: Make a number
As you and the children work through a range of activities related to each of the numerals to 10, let them use a variety of counting aids to make patterns of each number. Include among these pattern sets those made 'in steps' with Unifix®, Multilink® or similar apparatus.

Let the children use sticky paper shapes, colouring and printing to replicate these patterns. Make a display of the children's work. Numerals can be attached to the patterns made, to show addition and subtraction bonds.

Activity 2: Finish the pattern
Present children with patterned sequences of number bonds, where they have to complete the pattern or fill in the missing numbers. If they have mastered the steps in making numbers to 10 they should do these very quickly.

There are patterns of this kind to complete on **copymaster 52** (Number bonds).

Make 6

$5 + 1 =$
$4 + 2 =$
$3 + 3 =$
$2 + 4 =$
$1 + 5 =$

ODDS AND EVENS

C53, 54

Commentary
Mathematicians use a variety of means to sort numbers out, using ideas such as prime, square, cube, triangular and hexagonal numbers and so on. Odds and evens is one way which has been adopted in everyday life.

We feel that children should understand place value before trying to master odds and evens beyond 10. To say that 36 is an even number really means that you should not only know it is because the last digit is a 6 and that is divisible by 2, but that the whole number can be divided by 2.

Activity 1: Explaining odds and evens
Put out a small number of objects (for example, seven marbles) in front of a group of children. Ask: 'How many marbles are there? Can we put them into twos? Yes, there are three twos but there is an odd one left over. We say seven is an odd number.' Try again with, for example, four pencils. Tell the children that four is called an even number.

Invent a diagrammatic way to represent odds and evens. For example, you could draw a staircase with even numbers on the treads and odds on the risers, or they can be placed on a zigzag with odds at the bottom and evens at the top.

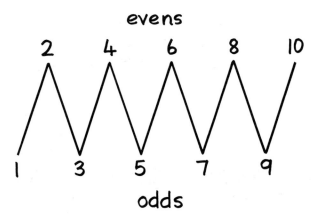

Activity 2: Oral odds and evens
As soon as you have introduced the concept of odd and even, the children can respond to oral work on these. They can play 'LOUD ODDS, quiet evens' while counting aloud to 20. They can sing the odds and 'growl' the evens! Ask a child to walk across the classroom. Note which is her or his leading foot, and then pin a label saying 'odd' to this foot. Attach an 'even' label to the other foot. Now ask her or him to walk across again while the children count aloud; the child's steps should match the odd and even labels.

Count aloud again and again, letting the children do a whole series of actions to rehearse the pattern of odds and evens; for example, putting their hands up for the odd numbers and/or putting their finger on their chin for even numbers. Let them have turns with a shaker or drum to make a sound when they hear an odd number.

Copymaster 53 (Odds and evens) presents the children with a sorting activity for odd and even numbers to 10.

60

Activity 3: Practice with odds and evens

Give the children some practical sorting activities, using odd and even numbers. For example, stick numbers onto cardboard houses, attach age badges to the toys and number some pictures of raffle prizes.

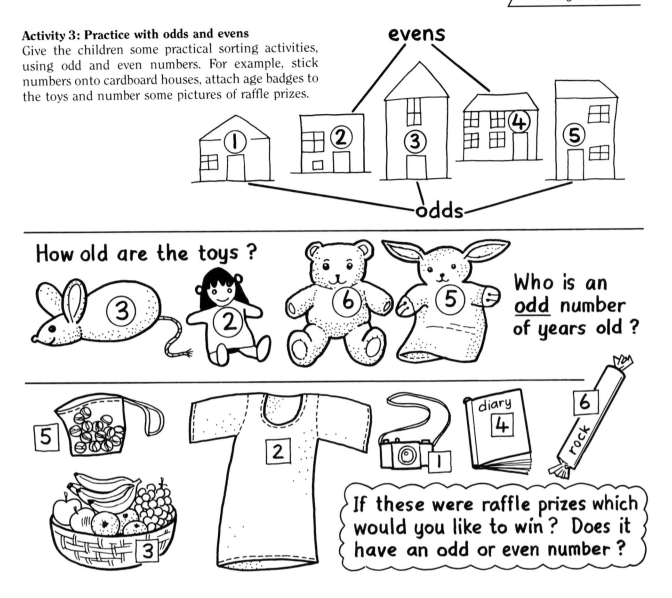

How old are the toys?

Who is an <u>odd</u> number of years old?

If these were raffle prizes which would you like to win? Does it have an odd or even number?

Copymaster 54 (Prize-winning numbers) lets the children identify odd and even numbers where the odds win a prize.

Activity 4: Numbers we know

Make a book of all the numbers that are important to the children, identifying which are odd and even. Each child may like to fill a page to add to a number book for all the class to look at.

Paula

There are 7 classes in school
7 is **odd**

I live at 6 Kings Road
6 is **even**

I have 2 gerbils
2 is **even**

SOLVING NUMBER MYSTERIES

C55

Commentary

Tell the children that mathematicians often use a letter of the alphabet to indicate missing information. The idea of finding this information from a set of clues underpins the solution of algebraic equations.

The use of function machines is a good way of exploring this part of algebra.

Activity 1: Maths mysteries using children
Explain to the children that mathematicians are often trying to find out what a mystery number is. Show the children a practical problem, using the children themselves as the resource, and work through it with them to demonstrate the idea that assembling all you know may enable you to find what is missing. Below is an example.

Try out some more problems using the children as a resource.

3 + ?

= 5

Activity 2: Maths mysteries using apparatus
Use counting aids and other equipment to create more 'missing number mysteries'. You could create a cardboard 'maths detective', or dress the class teddy in suitable clothes to identify the kinds of mysteries you are working on.

Create a display of number mysteries you have solved with the children, and set a new one out each day, that they can try when they have a moment to spare. Then at the end of each day work through it, or better still, ask one of the children who has solved it to explain how they did it. The problem can be added to a class dossier, which can go in the reading corner after the display is taken down.

Activity 3: What is the mystery number?
The problems can now be set out using conventional notation. Let the children use counting aids to work out the answers, but try not to let them lose the idea that it is a bit of detective work, as in Activities 1 and 2 above. When you mark their work, you can let the children know how many mysteries they have solved, that these cases are closed, and so on. Remember to give the children as wide a variety of layouts as possible. Here are some examples:

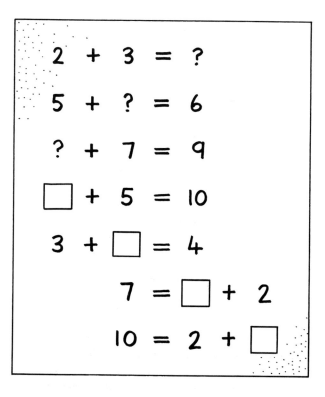

Copymaster 55 supplies some missing number mysteries.

62

PLAY AT MATHS DETECTIVE

C56
−8

Commentary

This final section presents some ideas for giving the children some independence in trying to solve problems.

One of the major difficulties in mathematics teaching is the general impression that mathematics is about finding one (right) solution. The preoccupation of many children, and adults, is getting the answer right. While it is important to be accurate and, where appropriate, provide the correct outcome of a computation, it is equally important that children come to see mathematics as exploratory and problems as being amenable to different approaches and solutions.

Activity 1: Robots

As an introduction to function machines place a big cardboard box on the floor. Cut two slots in it, one at each end. Let a child get into the box. Other children can post a numeral into one slot. The child in the box takes it and posts another numeral out of the other end. The children looking on have to decide what the 'function machine' has done to the number. You, as teacher, can record the operation of the function machine.

Let the children create their own robots using cartons and silver foil. They can set each other robot mysteries, by placing the 'secret' in the robot's tummy, and then showing their partner what number goes into one ear and what number comes out of the other! Make a display of the robots.

Copymasters 56 (An add 3 robot) and **57** (A take away 2 machine) present the children with some robot calculations.

Activity 2: Follow the number trail

Set a number trail in the classroom, where the children have to find out a mystery number at every stage. Let the children do this independently, when they have a few minutes, and record their final answer on a secrets chart (which can have anonymous entries). At the end of the day check through the trail with the children.

There is a number mini-trail on **copymaster 58** (Computation trail).

Activity 3: Laying a number trail

Let the children work in small groups to develop a missing number trail. They will need to draw up the prototype on a large sheet of paper, and then let you check it before laying a trail which some of their class-mates can try the following day.

REVIEW: ALGEBRA SO FAR

Experience of Level 2 algebra should empower the children in a number of ways. They should, for example, be able to:

● see patterns in number bonds to 10
● know which numbers are odd and which are even
● know what algebra is about, and that the starting principles are easy to understand
● show no reluctance in handling 'missing numbers'
● begin to organise mathematical data, in the pursuit of more information.

The important basics that we would see at this Level are:

● Extension of appreciation of number patterns
● Further understanding of the characteristics of numbers
● Foundations of functions
● Problem-solving strategies.

Attainment Target 3: Algebra, Level 3

Pupils should recognise and use symbolic and graphical representation to express relationships.

Programme of study	Statements of attainment	Examples
Pupils should engage in activities which involve:	Pupils should be able to:	Pupils could:
● developing a variety of strategies to perform mental calculations using number patterns and equivalent forms of two-digit numbers. ● explaining number patterns and predicting subsequent numbers. ● recognising whole numbers divisible by 2, 5 or 10.	a) Use pattern in number when doing mental calculations.	Continue: 5, 10, 15, 20 … Continue: $4 + 10 = 14$ $14 + 10 = 24$ $24 + 10 = 34$ … Find 27 + 31 by: $27 + 31 = 20 + 7 + 30 + 1$ $= 50 + 8$ $= 58$
● dealing with inputs to and outputs from simple function machines.	b) Use inverse operations in a simple context.	Use doubling and halving, adding and subtracting, and FORWARD and BACKWARD (in LOGO) etc, as inverse operations.

MENTAL COMPUTING MADE EASIER

C59
–61

Commentary

Give the children opportunities to break two-digit numbers into smaller numbers in order to make computation easier. For example, if 43 becomes 40 + 3, it may be easier to manipulate when adding another number to it.

The children should also be confident with approximation as a device for helping with calculations. If we know that 99 is very nearly 100, we can do a calculation with 99 in it as though it were 100, and make a deduction of 1 at the end to give the accurate answer.

Activity 1: Breaking down numbers

Practise breaking down numbers into tens and units, before doing complex additions and subtractions with a group of children. Work through some calculations as a group, then let the children do some individual recording.

There are calculations with space for breaking the numbers into tens and units on **copymasters 59** (Tens and units: addition) and **60** (Tens and units: subtraction).

Activity 2: Rough then right

Play approximations with the children. For example, they should be able to say that 28 is nearly 30 and 51 is close to 50. When they can do this unerringly, show them how this knowledge can be applied in calculations. Try working some through with the children and then let them work in pairs, and finally individually. At the end of each session, each child can choose a calculation and explain how they did it. A message from you at the bottom of their work, about the way they delivered their explanations, will help their confidence and their work in Attainment Target 1.

Copymaster 61 presents some calculations where approximation steps can be entered in.

Activity 3: All in the head

When the children are confident with the processes in Activities 1 and 2, they can try doing similar calculations in their heads. To have evidence of mental work you will need to ban counting aids, and ask the children to show you their answers. The children may find it helpful to use a two-stage operation, where they write their answers on the left-hand page in their book, get them marked, and then write down the steps they went through in their heads on the right-hand page.

PATTERN EXPLANATION AND PREDICTION

Commentary

The aim is that children should have a knowledge of number facts to 10, to the point where they can say them almost 'without thinking', or can work them out quickly, from their knowledge of the patterns formed by addition and subtraction to 10.

Class books and charts of number patterns should have as much appeal as poems or pictures. Do not deprive children of the pleasure of number by confining the patterns to worksheets or exercise books.

Activity 1: Oral number patterns

Quick-fire questions to the whole group, or individuals within it, will help the children to work out patterns in number facts to 10. Here are some examples:

● 'Today we are going to make seven. I shall give you a number and you can call out what we need to add to make seven. 0 ... 1 ... 2 ... 3 ... 4 ... 5 ... 6 ... 7 ... 3 ... 2 ... 5 ... 6', and so on.

● 'Do some "take away 2" calculations in your head. I shall say a number and you call out what that number less 2 is. 10 ... 9 ... 8 ... 7 ... 6 ... 5 ... (etc.) ... 10 ... 8 ... 6 ... 4', and so on.

● 'Give me a way of making 6 ... and another ... and another. Now make 6 using subtraction.'

Activity 2: Pattern layouts

Give the children the chance to record all the possible ways to make all the numbers up to 10, using addition and subtraction. It may be a good idea to have a class book of these.

If you have space for a 'number corner' you could use number patterns as one topic for a regular display. Mobiles, number strings, flap surprises, feely bags are some of the possible ways of displaying these.

Copymaster 62 presents some number pattern arrays for children to complete.

KNOW YOUR TABLES: TWOS, FIVES AND TENS

Commentary

This work ties in with that in Attainment Target 2, Level 3. The work on both Targets could be done at the same time.

The emphasis here is on the pattern of the numbers, and so it could be reinforced through pattern-making in art.

Activity 1: Multiply/divide by 2

Immerse the children in the pattern of twos. Have a pattern-making day and produce towers of twos, constructions of two strips/bricks, border patterns of twos, collage in twos, printing in twos, an ark and animals in twos. Make a '2' display and *The Story of 2* classbook.

Fill a resource box called 'Fun to do with 2', which could include colouring with shades of two colours, finding out about two kinds of big cat, asking two people with different views about what happens to grandma in Red Riding Hood, and creating birthday cakes for a second birthday.

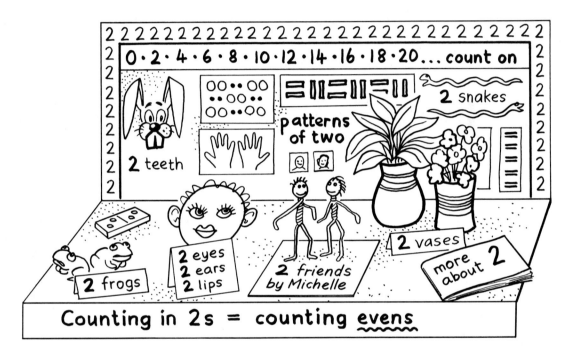

Activity 2: 'Two' rhymes

Collect these and teach them to the children. Include rhymes like 'Ten fat sausages' and 'Two, four, six, eight, who do we appreciate?'

Activity 3: Multiply/divide by 5

Repeat similar activities as Activity 1 above, including things like printing, collage and borders. Use squared paper (5 by 10 squares) to make patterns (**resource copymasters R4** and **R5** are for squared paper). Ask the children to invent rhymes and stories 'all about five'.

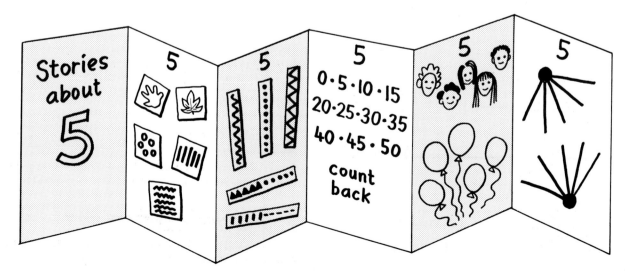

Activity 4: Multiply/divide by 10
Treat 10 in the way 2 and 5 are handled in Activities 1 and 3. Use hundred squares (**resource copymasters R2** and **R3**), coinage and notes, a Celsius thermometer scale, and number lines to highlight the pattern of tens.

Activity 5: Calculator play
Let the children make patterns of 2, 5, and 10 on the calculator.

FUNCTION MACHINES

C63
−6

Commentary
In work in Level 2 algebra the children met 'number robots'. This work is a continuation.

The use of function machines can fire children's motivation and allows them the chance to create their own machines. This reinforces a problem-solving and investigative approach to mathematics. It also provides children with a set of experiences which will open up work on graphs and relationships at a later stage.

Activity 1: Working function machines
Cut a piece out of either end of a small box (a box which once held tea bags, packet soup or cornflour is ideal) so that the box looks like a bridge. Mark one hole 'IN' and the other 'OUT'.

Place a piece of card under the box with, for example, '+2' on it. Now post a piece of card in the 'IN' side, with a numeral, for example 1, on it. Ask the children: 'If this was a machine and we posted in 1 and inside there was +2, what would we expect to come out?' When the children call out '3', place a piece of card with the numeral 3 on it near the 'OUT' hole.

Try this again, leaving the +2 card inside, and pushing in other numbers. The children will soon see that the 'machine' is a 'calculation machine'. Try changing the card inside, and try subtraction as well as addition cards. Tell the children that this is a function machine, and the function is what is happening to the number put in to get the number that comes out.

Copymasters 63 (An add 5 rocket), **64** (A take away 7 machine) and **65** (Star wars machines) give the children a chance to work out the outputs of function machines.

Activity 2: Finding the function
Try Activity 1 again, putting a mystery function inside the 'machine'. With the clues of some inputs and outputs the children should be able to determine what the function is.

Copymaster 66 (Mystery machines) presents some machines, and the children can find out what they might do.

Activity 3: Inventing function machines
Let the children make their own function machines from boxes or cartons and play at giving each other problems of these sorts:

● 'Here is what is in the machine, here is the number in, what is the number out?'
● (Put a function unseen into machine.) 'Here is the number in and the number out. What is the machine doing?'
● 'Keeping the same number in, what can we do to change the number out?'
● 'Keeping the same number out, what can we do to change the number in?'

LOGO

Commentary

LOGO is a computer language which is available in all primary schools. Unlike other programming languages it has been developed with young children in mind. The language that children need to learn in order to start to work in a LOGO environment is simple and short. As the children progress they can expand their knowledge of the available commands.

LOGO is a language which is geared to children controlling a symbol and causing it to move around the computer screen. As it does so it can leave a line of its path. This means that the children can construct all sorts of diagrams and pictures. The symbol they have to move around is a 'turtle'. There is now a range of robots available which respond to children's LOGO commands.

One particular quality of LOGO is that it is structured in such a way that children can teach the 'turtle' how to carry out sets of operations, and the 'turtle' will carry out these operations on command.

Of the instructions understood by LOGO on the computer, the following will allow the children to get started and will make it possible to produce a range of shapes:

FD (number) – forward the number of 'steps' given

BK (number) – backward the number of 'steps' given

RT (angle) – turn right the angle given
LT (angle) – turn left the angle given
CS – clear screen
PU – lift the 'pen' to stop drawing
PD – pen down to draw
PE – use the pen as an eraser

Activity: Introducing LOGO

For this activity you do not need any equipment. In the hall, play a 'guide your robot home' game with the children working in small groups. One child in each group plays the part of the robot 'turtle' and the others have to give the robot directions to travel from one part of the hall to another. Put obstacles such as hoops and/or skittles in the way so that they have to cope with instructing the robot to turn right and left as well as move forward or back particular numbers of steps.

So that the children can use the 'angle' instruction within LOGO, support them in making, for example, simple bearings discs based upon circular protractors. These need not include all degrees but, in the first instance, could have some of the more useful angles such as 90°, 45°, 60°.

If you have access to a real 'robot', use it to replicate the first robot game. Free-standing robots now available will allow children to program them to move, turn and even play tunes. With a pen attachment they can also draw a path on large sheets of paper.

REVIEW: ALGEBRA SO FAR

In children's learning, the foundations of algebra are laid down in three ways. These are by:

● exploring pattern
● grouping numbers by particular, named characteristics
● learning that something needs to be done to a number to change it to another number.

All of these build upon work in number and all need practical activity to give them meaning. Algebra should not be seen as being about learning formulae and the tricks for manipulating equations. Both formulae and equations come out of generalisations of particular cases. Algebra seeks to simplify, not confuse! Of all of the activities listed in this section we would draw particular attention to the potential in function machines and in the use of LOGO. Both are readily available but both are under-used. This is a pity for both offer highly motivating learning opportunities to children, and their teachers.

Attainment Target 4: Shape and space

Pupils should recognise and use the properties of two-dimensional (2-D) and three-dimensional (3-D) shapes and use measurement, location and transformation in the study of space.

Shape and space is one of the two major building blocks of mathematics, the other being *number*. It is possible to express an awareness of two- and three-dimensional relationships without a sophisticated number system. Prehistoric cave paintings illustrate this point very well, as do early examples of sculpture and carving. Early measurements were done with locally produced units which often used the human body as a 'rule of thumb'. But trade between communities, combined with a growing desire to understand more about natural phenomena, led to the introduction of standard units of measurement. It is important, in order for children to grasp the meaning of standard units, for them to emulate their ancestors and gain experience in creating and using their own units of measurement.

In studying shape and space, children and adults are opening up their appreciation of a range of relationships to do with the natural and designed worlds. Starting from an appreciation of ourselves as having a three-dimensional existence we can move outwards to relationships with others, expressed perhaps in dance or sport. We can locate ourselves, our home, our town through maps and mapping to our country and our location on the planet Earth. Earth in space, galaxies and the universe all become part of our understanding of spatial relationships. We can take our appreciation of relationships and patterns within ourselves right down to the molecules and atoms of which all matter is made.

Shape and space, then, is not a matter of being able to identify a limited range of named shapes such as triangles and squares – although the acquisition of this sort of knowledge is important in that it allows an analysis of complex patterns in terms of constituent shapes. Shape and space work should be seen as offering experience from which children can produce increasingly more sophisticated constructions and analyses of two- and three-dimensional structures.

Resourcing shape and space
In addition to the equipment listed in the resource bank at the front of the book, the following will be useful in work on shape and space:

● Paper, with squares of different sizes, 'dotty' papers (see **resource copymasters R4–R7**)
● Constructional materials ranging from paper and plastic straws through to some sets of commercially produced constructional equipment
● Accurate mathematical shapes like Logiblocks® or Poleidoblocs® and shape templates of different shapes and in different colours, including quadrilaterals (some of which are rectangles and squares), circles and ellipses, triangles (some of which are right-angled), pentagons and hexagons
● Plasticised mirrors
● A collection of natural and designed objects demonstrating a range of shapes and posters showing examples of designed and natural structures (e.g. bridges and beehives)
● Magnetic compasses, compass designs like those on maps, a weather vane and a globe
● Set-squares with different angles.

Collections of cartons and packaging should include cubes and cuboids (boxes), cylinders (drinking straws, dowel, cylindrical containers), prisms (chocolate boxes). Add to these a sphere (table tennis ball, marbles, globe), a cone (ice-cream wafer) and a pyramid (home-made or chocolate box). Work in shape and space connects with work in science, technology and art, and materials for these areas of the curriculum will also be useful in mathematics.

In addition to all these things the following will help with specific activities in this section:

● Screws, screwdrivers, screw-top jars, keys, clock-work toys
● Sand trays, a tambour, feely bags
● An Anglepoise lamp, angle iron, information books about angled decks on aircraft and angular distance
● LOGO software and 'turtle' robot
● Books about pattern
● Plastic and real coins
● Rules and tapes (both metric and imperial)
● Containers of different shapes and volumes, and measuring jugs
● Kitchen scales and bathroom scales.

Attainment Target 4: Shape and space, Level 1

Pupils should recognise and use the properties of two-dimensional (2-D) and three-dimensional (3-D) shapes and use measurement, location and transformation in the study of space.

Programme of study	Statements of attainment	Examples
Pupils should engage in activities which involve:	Pupils should be able to:	Pupils could:
• sorting and classifying 2-D and 3-D shapes using words such as 'straight', 'flat', 'curved', 'round', 'pointed', etc.	a) Talk about models they have made.	*Make various constructions, models or pictures from a range of materials and describe them.*
• building 3-D solid shapes and drawing 2-D shapes and describing them.		
• using common words, such as 'on', 'inside', 'above', 'under', 'behind', 'next to', to describe a position.		
• giving and understanding instruction for movement along a route.	b) Follow or give instructions related to movement and position.	*Follow directions in a PE lesson, or on an errand around school.*
		Follow signed instructions or cards displaying symbols for 'over', 'under', 'on', 'in', etc. in using an obstacle course or maze in PE.
		In ☐ Over ☐
		On ☐ Under ☐
		Give instructions to direct a simple programmable toy.
• comparing objects and ordering objects and events without measuring, using appropriate language.	c) Compare and order objects without measuring.	*Use language such as 'long', 'longer than', 'longest'; 'tall', 'taller' than', 'tallest'; 'heavy', 'light'; 'before', 'after'.*

NOTICING AND NAMING SHAPES ▶

Commentary

The intentions here are two-fold. First, the children should be made aware of some of the shapes around them, and reminded of what they know about these shapes. As you are 'raising awareness' try not to limit the kinds of responses children make. All that they can say about a shape will help to enlarge their intellectual map of that shape.

Secondly, you are beginning an induction of the children into new perspectives and new ways of describing their world. It does have some jargon attached, and so they do need to learn the mathematical names for shapes. However, the name for a shape and its distinguishing features (which children will have the opportunity to learn at Level 2) are but a small part of what children need to know.

Work with small groups where possible, because all the children will want a 'go' and it is important that they handle the shapes in collections and on displays.

Technically speaking, a thin flat plastic shape and a shape drawing on paper are not two-dimensional, for the plastic has thickness, as does the ink and paper. Except for high precision work in, for example, micro-engineering, we accept 'flat' shapes as two-dimensional.

Activity 1: Shape awareness

Ask the children what they understand by 'shape' and discuss with them some of the shapes they know. They may have idiosyncratic ways of naming shapes and of comparing them. Collect together and discuss all the words they use, including things like 'lumpy', 'curvy', 'pointed' and even emotive words like 'scary', 'kind', 'comfortable'. Record the discussions in a concertina book or chart for the start of a display.

Activity 2: Matching 3-D shapes
From your shape and space resource box take a number of real cartons and containers. Now play games like these:

● *Match the shape* – Pick one up and the children can pick one out to match.
● *Which shape is missing?* – Take away a shape, while the children close their eyes, and they point to one like the one missing.
● *Create a feely bag* (a borrowed shoe bag works well) and place a shape or collection of shapes in the bag unseen. The children can take it in turns to try to match a shape on the table with a shape in the bag, either by feeling through the fabric of the bag or by putting their hand inside.

Include in the collection at least the following shapes, though the children may not need to name them all at this level:

> Cuboid
> Cube
> Cylinder
> Prisms with triangular and
> hexagonal bases
> Sphere
> Cone.

When not in use lay the shapes out on a display table so that the children can handle them.

Activity 3: Naming 2-D shapes
Assemble a collection of two-dimensional shapes, including the following, though the children may not be able to name them all:

> Rectangle
> Square
> Circle
> Triangle
> Hexagon
> Pentagon.

Play games similar to those in Activity 2. Mount a display where the shapes can be touched when not in use, and named, if you feel the children are ready to name them.

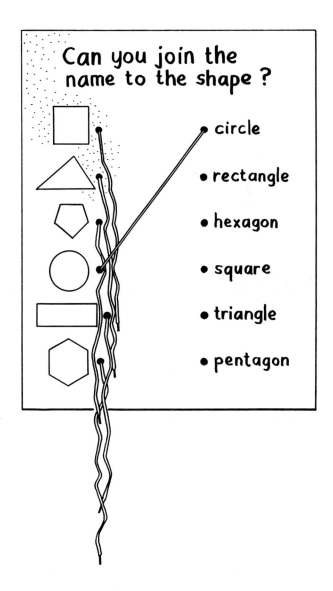

Activity 4: Shapes around the school
Let the children look around the school, both inside and out, and spot as many shapes as they can. They can have a go at first recording by drawing some of the shapes they see on paper. For a report-back session have a large sectioned piece of paper ready. You can then label the children's sketches and cut them out to assemble in the set of the correct shape.

Give the children a little picture quiz called 'Find the shape'. Tell them where the answers are likely to be – not too far away from the classroom! You could include, for example, a drawing of the framed picture in the corridor, the caretaker's broomstick, the door to the playground and the shape of the window.

Activity 5: Shape collections

Create a shape collecting point, and invite children to bring in packaging suitable for junk modelling. When you have a mountain of shapes, let the children sort them out. Choose the best examples for the resource box and put the others aside for some of the activities to come.

Start a collection of natural shapes which the children can handle. Include, for example, a blown egg, a starfish, angular pieces of rock, a hollow log, a palmate leaf, a snail shell. In fact you can include any natural shape which will get the children talking and collecting.

Arrange a complementary display of manufactured shapes. These could include a sole for a shoe, a piece of raw spaghetti, plastic tubing, a cardboard box, a plastic bottle, a kite, coins, a belt and a headscarf.

BUILDING 3-D SHAPES

Commentary

Before children learn about maths they almost all have had experience of building *with* shapes, which is the place to begin this part of their work. However, you need to be aware that because of traditional expectations and stereotyping, some girls may have not had much opportunity for constructional play. Boys are still the ones who are commonly and routinely given construction opportunities.

It is worth giving children support in junk model-making, partly because they can talk and learn while they work and also because cartons turned inside out and re-stuck (by an adult) take paint reasonably well and look much more attractive.

Activity 1: Building *with* shapes

Provide the children with a wide range of three-dimensional shapes with which to build. You can do much with junk modelling materials, and the pleasure in these is that they form an eye-catching display, a talking point for you and the children (for example: 'What shape is the wheel on Ernie's tractor?') and they can be taken home.

Duplo®, Lego®, Multilink®, wooden bricks, and other commercially available construction toys can be used to good effect in temporary model-making. There are also sets of building shapes on the market which children love to play with and have the features of 'mathematical' shapes. Poliedoblocs® is one such commercially available set.

Activity 2: Building cuboids and cubes

Lego® is the obvious resource to use. Many of the pieces are cuboid (if you ignore the dimples), and solid and hollow cuboids can be made using them.

Lego® or wooden blocks can give children the opportunity to construct cubes. When they have played, give them challenges like: 'Can you build a smaller one? How many pieces do you think are in the shape you have built?'.

Activity 3: Building cylinders

Curl paper and ribbon and let the children make paper sculptures.

Let the children try making a cylinder shape from heavy rope. Display this and then show them how to decorate an empty tin (with a safe top edge) with coloured wools and strings. Let the children make play paper telescopes and clay coil pots.

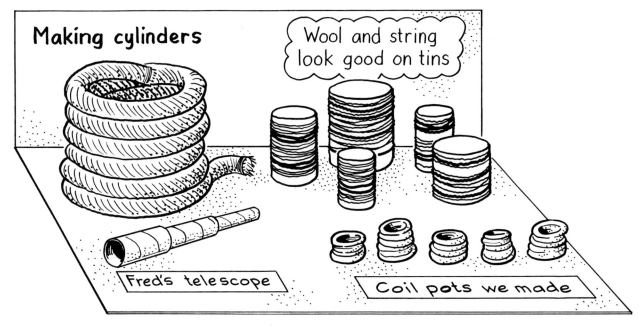

Activity 4: Building prisms
These shapes are quite hard to build. Try using strips of card, folded to match a size strip. Fold into shape and stick. They will then make good collages or mobiles, or could be stuck together to make a tunnel or roof.

Activity 5: Building spheres
Play dough, Plasticine® and clay are possible media here. You can also try cooking things like raspberry buns and ginger nuts where the dough has to be rolled into balls before being placed on the baking sheet.

Activity 6: Skeleton shapes
Using Artstraws® or paper drinking straws, help the children to make a few skeleton shapes, including a cube, a cuboid and a pyramid. The children may find this difficult without adult help.

There are construction sets available which may be easier for the children to handle; they include plastic straws and connectors.

Activity 7: Irregular shapes
When the opportunity arises point out to the children that not all shapes are regular, but that they need to have certain features to belong to a shape family. This is laying the foundations for work at Level 2.

DRAWING 2-D SHAPES

Commentary
Children's hand control skills may be limited when they are ready for this work. They should, however, be able to do a rough but recognisable sketch of shapes they see. This is quite adequate at this stage.

There is a challenge for you to find as many ways of recording shape, other than drawing, as you can.

Activity 1: 'Magic finger' drawing
Ask the children to draw shapes as you draw them, with a 'magic finger' in the air. Draw with fingers in other media, like sand and chalk dust.

What shapes have we drawn in the sand trays?

Diane   Len

Activity 2: Draw what you see

Show the children a collection of card or plastic shapes and let them draw what they see. They can create pictures composed entirely of the shapes on the table.

Copymaster 67 (Shape pictures) is a drawing sheet using shape.

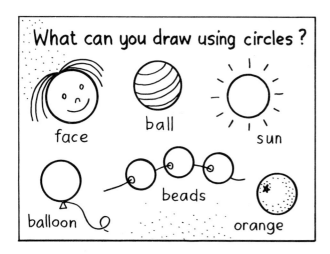

Activity 3: Drawing round

Give the children the same kinds of shapes as in Activity 2 above and let them draw round them to produce pictures. Set the children open-ended challenges like: 'Draw a monkey, or a petrol station, or a playground.' Also set some that are structured; for example, 'Draw a supermarket shelf of food using rectangles and squares, or a nest of chicks using circles and ovals.'

Activity 4: Painting and printing

Paint shapes with fingers and brushes, using powder paint, water colours, fluorescent paint. Rub a candle really hard over a shape under a piece of paper – colour wash over it and the shape will appear. Paint sequences

of shapes to make border designs and repeat patterns. Try painting a single shape in different positions and using different colours.

Print with sponges, boxes, ends of cylinders, coins (stuck on boxes), wooden sticks, ends of pencils and pen tops. Produce repeat patterns, patterns of size, borders and random patterns. Create galaxies and bubble baths, building sites and boxes of toys, aviaries and shelves of books. The children's art links shape and space and pattern to the real world.

Activity 5: Sticky shapes

Use ready-cut sticky shapes to produce pictures, patterns and mosaics. The latter is a direct experience of tessellation which the children will tackle at Level 6.

75

DESCRIBING POSITION

Commentary

Explore the language we use to describe position. The first steps in such an exploration are to start with a few variables. Here we are concerned with a discussion of fixed positions and not the movement between one position and another.

Activity 1: Position words

The children will already know many position words. Play guessing games like 'Where is the book?' 'Where is the doll?' 'Where is the headteacher?' Encourage the children to use words like:

    up/down
    under/over
    above/below
    beside
    in front of/behind
    on top of/underneath.

Ask two children to stand facing the others. Move the children's hands or legs into position and tell the class: 'Tracy's leg is beside Hannah's. Hannah's hand is above Tracy's', and so on. Then give Hannah and Tracy directions, so that they can move into position to match the instructions.

Ask the group of children to work in pairs, and give one of each pair a red sticker. The others should have a blue sticker. Now give directions to the whole group. For example, you may say, 'Blues stand in front of reds. Reds crouch down while blues stand up.'

Put all this position vocabulary into a classbook and add it to the book corner.

Activity 2: Position quiz

Make a set of simple picture clues that match to things around the room. Ask the children, a pair at a time, to find where the clues go.

To help recognition, **copymaster 68** (Position words) is a set of pictures with position words attached which the children can ring.

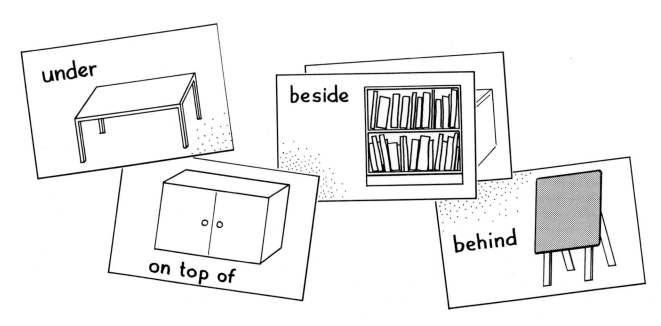

MOVING POSITION

Commentary

Here we start to combine position vocabulary with movement. In moving it is important to stress the idea of *rotation*. This is in order to give the children a good platform for when they encounter the idea of an angle.

Activity 1: Position in PE and dance

During PE lessons, plan work specifically to cover position words. Starter games include 'Statues' and 'Machines'. Once the children have had a few sessions at exploring these, you can begin to set quite detailed limits to the position they adopt when you stop their movement by giving a clap. For example, you could say: 'I should like you to move around as fast as you can, and when I clap I want you to be a statue looking up and pushing down' or 'When I clap, the machine must do two lifting-up movements and then stop.'

Help the children to invent a simple dance routine based on a few position words, set it to music and work it into an assembly called perhaps 'Going shopping' or 'Exploring the jungle.'

Activity 2: Position in play

In the play activities set for the children, you can ensure that there is a full range of position words, and directions to change position.

Activity 3: Program a robot

Let the children have a go at giving instructions to a programmable robot (there are a number available through educational suppliers). See if the children can get the robot to follow a route describing a shape, or master a simple obstacle course.

TALKING ABOUT MEASURES

Commentary

This introduction to measures begins with a look at some of the everyday words we use in making comparisons of the following: dimensions, area, weight, capacity, temperature, monetary value, time and other differences. The intention is that the children should be confident with the language of measurement before they record.

Measurement is about comparison. We would say a beach ball is big when compared with a golf ball, but the golf ball is said to be big when compared with a marble. What we should be saying each time is 'bigger than'. Do not be tempted to make collections of 'light' things or 'small' things, though there can in a collection be things that are 'lighter than . . .' and you can declare something the 'lightest' on the table. Everyday comparisons are idiosyncratic, and depend on context. You depend on a common understanding of what you imply. A bag of sugar might be pronounced heavy by a five-year-old, but an adult in weight-training would not say the same. Encourage the children with their 'comparison' vocabulary, even with dimensions which

they will probably not measure and quantify in the infant school, like flexibility and hardness. Work like this will reinforce measurement as being a comparison exercise, and will help their work in other subjects (for example, science AT 3, and technology).

Note that, at this stage, all is talk and 'play'. Do not make the children write anything down yet!

Activity 1: Size and coverage

Talk about size. Start with an object, for example a toy mouse or a fir cone, and discuss with the children things that are bigger than or smaller than these. You could focus the discussion by comparing the mouse with other animals they know, and the fir cone with other fruits. Continue the discussion in a series of sessions, using objects and pictures of objects, gradually exploring the vocabulary with the children. Do not forget to try a series of cloths on the play house table to see which covers it, and paper masks which may cover the face. This is just to 'set the scene' for later discussions of area.

Collect all the common words we use in talking about size. These may include:

- big/bigger/biggest, large/larger/largest
- small/smaller/smallest, little/littler/littlest
- tiny/tinier/tiniest
- long/longer/longest, short/shorter/shortest
- tall/taller/tallest, wide/wider/widest
- broad/broader/broadest
- narrow/narrower/narrowest
- thin/thinner/thinnest, fat/fatter/fattest
- high/higher/highest, low/lower/lowest.

Make a class folder or book with all these words in it. Develop the concepts further in the activities under 'Compare and order' below.

Activity 2: How heavy?

As in Activity 1, use a collection of objects to elicit everyday words about 'weight' from the children. These will include the following:

- weigh, balance, scales, pointer, dial
- light/lighter/lightest, heavy/heavier/heaviest.

Make a class folder of key words, for use in 'Compare and order' opposite.

Activity 3: How much will it hold?

Play with sand and water provides opportunities to talk about the following:

- How much? How many fill . . . ? full/empty
- more/most, less/least.

Class charts or folders will help children to recognise, use and later record the appropriate vocabulary.

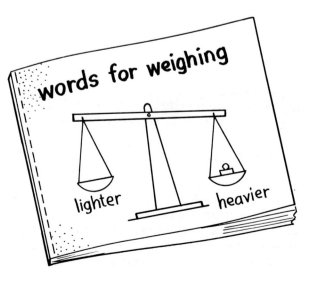

78

Activity 4: Hot or cold?

Use the weather and how we feel, what we and our pets do in summer and winter, and a collection of objects including, for example, a warm drink, a hot water bottle with warm water in it, and metal or stone which is cold to the touch. Talk about hot and cold and establish the vocabulary of temperature, including:

- hot/hotter/hottest, cold/colder/coldest
- warm/warmer/warmest, cool/cooler/coolest.

Add these words to the class measures folder.

Activity 5: What is it worth?

Let the children look at money under a magnifier, and talk about and compare real coins and notes (from your purse!). Let them compare these with the play money they use for their money work at school. Look at the value written on each coin and lay them out in order.

Activity 6: Early or late?

The school day can be a starting point for talk about time and timing, including:

- school times, kinds of clocks, clock face, hands, timing in sport
- early/earlier/earliest, late/later/latest
- before/after, hours/o'clock.

Annotated clock books are useful additions to the book corner.

Activity 7: How hard/flexible/transparent/recyclable is it?

Assemble a variety of materials which the children can handle and make judgements about. Their observations do not need to be exhaustive, but they should get plenty of practice in making comparisons. You could include, for example, wool, stone, plastic, wood, newspaper, chalk, metal, cotton fabric and cardboard.

COMPARE AND ORDER

C69, 70

Commentary

This work can follow on from or tie in with 'Talking about measures' above.

As with number, start with the children themselves. They are the most readily available resource, and will be motivated when they are both learner and teaching aid. Be sensitive to the children's feelings about their characteristics. To be the shortest or to have the biggest family or ears in the group may be embarrassing to a child. Think before you encourage the children to make these comparisons.

Note that we have put 'weight' in quotation marks, because what we measure in this way is actually mass. We shall, however, use the word 'weight' as it is what we say in everyday speech.

Activity 1: Ourselves

Let the children make comparisons between one another. Invite three children of differing heights to stand in front of the others and ask the rest to call out in answer to, for example: 'Who is the tallest?' (Hal) 'Who is the shortest?' (Tony) 'How many people are taller than Charlene?' (One, Hal) 'Who is wearing the longest sleeves?' (Tony) 'Who has the most buttons?' (Charlene) Compare the children's hair length. (Charlene's is the longest, Hal's the shortest. Tony's hair is longer than Hal's and shorter than Charlene's. Two people have hair shorter than Charlene's. Two people have hair longer than Hal's. And so on).

Compare a variety of characteristics, choosing two, three or more children for the comparisons. You could compare, for example:

- hair, noses, ears, eyes, specs
- sleeves, collars, buttons, lengths of skirts or trousers
- shoe sizes, hand sizes.

Hal   Tony   Charlene

Activity 2: Things around us

Try to bring in as wide a range of things as possible for comparisons, including things smaller than a shirt button (perhaps an apple pip or honesty seed), covering more ground than the classroom (perhaps the

Arrange comparison displays in the classroom and let all the children contribute and take turns at arranging them, or deciding the comparisons.

hall or playing field), longer than a skipping rope (maybe the school fence!) and bigger than the head-teacher's car (perhaps the swimming coach or minibus).

Copymaster 69 (Measuring vocabulary) offers a simple record of some comparisons.

fruits in order of size

Here are some more things to sort:

pieces of material   empty boxes   toys with wheels

Sonia and Madhur made the display

80

Activity 3: Things we know about
Invite the children to make more comparisons on the basis of information about themselves and their friends – for example (even if they boast!), the sizes of their appetites, their bedtimes, and the sizes of their pets are all starting points for comparisons.

Copymaster 70 (Comparing measurements) allows a record of some comparisons between a child and two friends.

Ellie, Angela and Win compared their pets

| Angela's pony 'Star' is biggest | Win's hamster 'Blotch' is smallest | Ellie's cat 'Toots' is smaller than 'Star' and bigger than 'Blotch' |

PLAYING MEASURING

 C71

Commentary
Role play is discussed in the section on number. We have used the same settings here to give children specific experience of measures.

Activity 1: Play house
Size play may include a comparison with things in children's own homes, in the play house and in a dolls' house. The three bears can inhabit the play house for a few days while the children assemble, order and compare all their belongings. If the class does not have

three bears as resources, make them out of card. They can be made to stand in the house and have paper clothes put on them like paper dolls.

The children can set out the bears' bowls, beds, spoons, paw prints and other characteristics.

Time play may include a list of 'jobs' to do in the house, with discussion of 'before' and 'after'. The dolls could have a play timetable, devised and carried through by the children.

Activity 2: Play shop or restaurant
The play shop can have a range of contents, for example like those we mentioned in the section on number. Another possibility which may give a range of learning opportunities is a restaurant. Here are some ideas to set the business going:

● Size of plate, portion, table, cloth
● Capacity of teapot, jug, cup, glass, bottle (all plastic)
● 'Weight' of meat in burger (the children may know about quarter pounders) or steak.

The 'customers' could comment on the food, either in a group discussion or on paper. This may be their first recording of comparisons. The comment sheet could say, for example, 'Draw what you had to eat. Was it less (or more) than you eat at home? Are the portions smaller (or bigger) than you like?' Display the children's comments and suggestions, highlighting all the measurement vocabulary they are using.

This work can be dramatised to make part of an entertaining assembly.

Copymaster 71 (Restaurant comments) is a 'customer comments' sheet for the restaurant.

Activity 3: Play post office
A play post office gives opportunities for playing with coins, and comparing the weights of parcels.

Activity 4: Play spaceship
Equip your spaceship for a two-day trip. Collect empty packets, cans, bottles, wrappers, etc. 'How much food and drink will you need to take? How much luggage space will it take up? Can the space travellers fit in too?'

REVIEW: SHAPE AND SPACE SO FAR ▶

All the activities we have talked about have dealt with shape in the real world. Ask children to put their developing concepts to use in their model-making and art work. For example: 'What shape is best for a cot? Why is that?' 'Can you make a tunnel or tower with a platform from Lego®? What shapes will you need to make it? What shape will it be when it is finished?' Let them work on paper that is not rectangular, and get them to explore the spaces between shapes as well as the shapes themselves. The messages are that the exploration of shape and space should be based on practical activity and centred on investigative approaches.

Work at this level should ensure that the children have at their fingertips:

● the vocabulary of shape
● the vocabulary of position
● an intellectual map of common two- and three-dimensional shapes

● an understanding of change in position.

They should also be using their vocabulary and concepts in viewing, describing and explaining the world in terms of shape.

In introducing young children to measures, the priorities are to do with the essentials of comparison and the associated vocabulary that goes with these comparisons. At Level 1 the basics are:

● comparisons in time, weight, length, volume and money
● much talk about measurements and the use of the vocabulary of comparative measures.

It is essential that this work is not rushed. Without the concepts of scale that comparisons embody, work in such areas as estimation and accurate measurement will be made extremely difficult at later Levels.

Attainment Target 4: Shape and space, Level 2

Pupils should recognise and use the properties of two-dimensional (2-D) and three-dimensional (3-D) shapes and use measurement, location and transformation in the study of space.

Programme of study	Statements of attainment	Examples
Pupils should engage in activities which involve:	Pupils should be able to:	Pupils could:
• recognising squares, rectangles, circles, triangles, hexagons, pentagons, cubes, rectangular boxes (cuboids), cylinders and spheres and describing their properties. • recognising right-angled corners in 2-D and 3-D shapes.	a) Use mathematical terms to describe common 2-D shapes and 3-D objects.	*Create pictures and patterns using 2-D shapes and describe them. Describe 3-D objects using appropriate language.*
• recognising types of movement: straight (translation), turning (rotation). • understanding angle as a measurement of turn. • understanding turning through right angles. • understanding the conservation of length, capacity and 'weight'.	b) Recognise different types of movement.	*Rotate body through 1, 2, 3 and 4 right angles. Turn to left or right on instructions (in PE, games using turtle graphics or programmable toys).*

2-D SHAPES

C72
–4

Commentary
With work at Level 1 covered thoroughly, the children should sail through these activities. They offer an opportunity for you to consolidate work at Level 1 and identify any children who have not yet truly grasped some of the basic principles.

Activity 1: The language of shape
Both you and the children will probably use words other than shape names in your mathematical discussions. Now is the opportunity to ensure that the children fully understand a wide range of words used in talking about shapes.
 Introduce all of these to the children:

● corner (and, if they arise, point, vertex)
● side (2-D) and edge (3-D)
● face
● three-dimensional ('back', 'front' and 'thickness')
● two-dimensional (no 'thickness').

 Place a number of boxes and cartons or plastic or card shapes on the table, and ask a child to point to, for example, one with four corners, one with more than four faces, a shape with six sides and so on. The children will enjoy setting this kind of problem for one another.

Activity 2: Shapes in class
Now that the children have some maths language for shapes and their features, you can encourage them to look for shapes around the room. Ask them to work in pairs to spot as many of one shape as they can in a couple of minutes. Assemble their results by drawing sketches of what they spotted, or combining these with pictures cut from magazines.

Activity 3: Work with squares and rectangles

Use a collection of flat plastic shapes, which should include a number of squares and rectangles and irregular quadrilaterals and parallelograms. From these the children, working in a small group, can make selections. Choose a square from the collection, and without saying what it is called, ask each child to find another like it. If the children can name it, ask them to tell you about it. A child may say, 'It has four corners.' You can then pick up an irregular quadrilateral and ask, 'Is this a square?' Gradually the children will be able to say what the key attributes are that identify a square (namely four sides of equal length and four corners the same).

Now play the same game, choosing a rectangle from the collection, and eventually helping the children to understand that a rectangle has two pairs of sides with equal lengths and four corners the same.

Start a shape identifier book.

Activity 4: Work with triangles

Use a collection of triangles cut from card and plastic. Make sure there is a range including equilateral (sides of equal length), right-angled and some with very acute angles. Add a few shapes that are not triangles to the collection. Using the same game as in Activity 1 help the children to establish what the crucial attributes of a triangle are (namely that it has three sides!). You do not need to ask the children to distinguish between kinds of triangles at this stage.

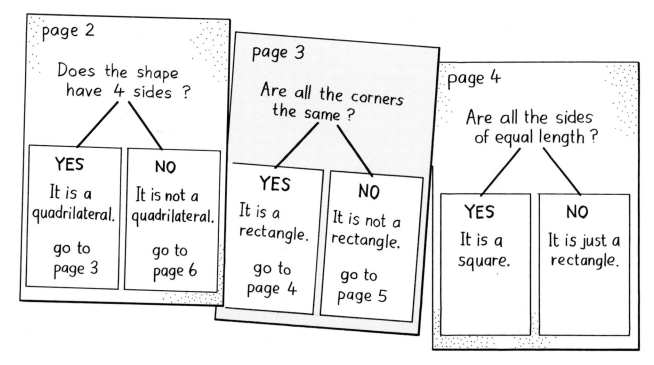

Activity 5: Work with circles
Use a collection of circles, ovals and ellipses for this game. Just ensure that the children can pick out a circle from a collection. They need only be able to distinguish it at this stage, and not name its attributes.

Activity 6: Work with hexagons and pentagons
Create a collection of shapes with many sides and of varying sizes. Include hexagons and pentagons. If the children can pick these shapes out of the collection,

see if they can identify the attribute they are using to choose the appropriate shape. If they cannot choose the appropriate shape, take one yourself, name it, and get the children to find one that matches. Talk together about how to find this shape among others.

Copymasters 72–74 let the children match attributes to shapes. **Copymasters 73 and 74** should be photocopied on to card, and the small cards on copymaster 74 cut out; a child can then match these to the attributes printed on the board of copymaster 73.

3-D SHAPES

Commentary

The children may be familiar with some of the names of these shapes, though they may have forgotten the word 'cuboid' as it is not used very often in everyday speech.

Check that the children are confident about using shape vocabulary, including 'face', 'side', 'edge' and 'corner'.

There are, in fact, only five *regular* three-dimensional shapes. We do not intend that you should teach the children these shapes but it is important to see the direction of some aspects of three-dimensional work. The regular solids are:

● *Cube.* Six faces, each face being a square. Three faces meet at each corner or vertex.
● *Tetrahedron.* Four faces, each face being an equilateral triangle. Three faces meet at each vertex.
● *Octahedron.* Eight faces, each face being an equilateral triangle. Four faces meet at each vertex. (A regular octahedron can be made by sticking two similar square-based pyramids together, whose edges are all equal.)
● *Icosahedron.* Twenty faces, each face being an equilateral triangle. Five faces meet at each vertex.
● *Dodecahedron.* Twelve faces, each face being a pentagon. Three faces meet at each vertex.

A sphere shares with the regular solids the characteristic that its shape does not change, you just get larger or smaller versions of spheres. But spheres do not have plane faces. When you take a section across a sphere the plane cut is always a circle.

Activity 1: Work with cubes and cuboids

From the resource box assemble a collection of cartons, boxes and mathematical shapes which are shaped like a cube or cuboid. The children may be able to sort out the cubes and say what distinguishes them from the other shapes.

Make a list of all the things the children know that come in cube shapes. Add these to a class chart or display.

Now do the same activity with cuboids. Finally set a cube beside a cuboid and look for differences.

Copymaster 75 presents some work on cubes and cuboids.

Activity 2: Work with cylinders

From the resource box assemble a collection of cylinders. To the ubiquitous paper roll centres and chocolate bean containers, do not forget to add a piece of dowel and a broomstick! Ask the children to look at what distinguishes a cylinder from other shapes. See if they can predict what a cylinder will look like if it is laid out flat. Cut and open out a paper cylinder to show them. Arrange a display to include some cylinders that children may have failed to notice.

Copymaster 76 presents some work with cylinders.

85

Activity 3: Work with spheres

Not many things are packaged in spherical containers. If they fill a box with cuboids, and then with spheres the children may be able to work out why that is. Balls of Plasticine®, marbles, a football, a tennis ball and a globe will be a big enough collection for children to examine. You do not need to discuss the properties of spheres further at this stage.

Add the spheres to the classroom display for a while.

Copymasters C77–79 provide a game for two to four players based on recognition of two-dimensional representations of three-dimensional shapes. Photocopy all three masters on to card. Cut up the shape cards on copymaster C79 and the four game boards on copymasters C77 and C78. Place the shape cards face down, spread over the table (as in 'Memory match' games). Each player in turn picks up one card; if it is one they need for the model on their game board, they keep it; otherwise, they replace the card on the table. The winner is the first player to collect all the shapes needed for their model.

A collection of spheres

RIGHT ANGLES

C80, 81

Commentary

It can be quite difficult to draw a shape without using a right angle. Right angles are extremely common in the built environment. 'Square' corners occur everywhere, and this makes it the best choice for starting work with the children on the notion of angle.

Activity 1: Introducing right angles

Folding a piece of paper in half and then in half again will produce a right angle. Do this with the children and tell them about the angle's special name. Ask them to search around the classroom to see where there are right angles. Compile a list of the right angles that they can find. Talk about the characteristics of a right angle after this activity.

Copymaster 80 gives practice in recording right angles.

Activity 2: Right angle search

Using two- and three-dimensional shapes from the shape resource box, let the children examine them to find right angles. They should now be able to say that squares, rectangles, cubes and cuboids all have right-

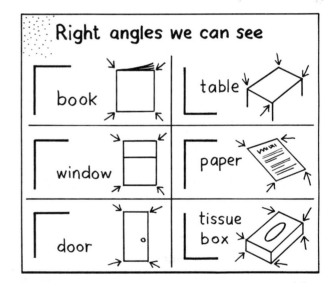

Right angles we can see

book · table · window · paper · door · tissue box

angled corners, and some triangles and prisms do too.

Arrange a sorting display where the children can add to sets of shapes which have and lack right angles.

Copymaster 81 gives practice in identifying shapes with right angles.

These have right angles

These do not

MOVEMENT

Commentary

Now is the time to set the groundwork for work on symmetry at Level 3 and beyond.

Work on movement can tie in with ideas related to repeat patterns in algebra.

Underlying our power to conserve length, capacity and weight is an understanding of position and orientation, which can be developed through moving ourselves and objects around us.

Activity 1: Kinds of movement in PE

During a series of PE lessons, explain to the children the kinds of movement there are. These can be named:

● *Straight movement* (translation). Marching might be seen as a straight movement.
● *Turning movement* (rotation). Ballet-type dance and graceful flowing movements involve turning of the limbs and whole body.

Include in the activities a series of movements, some involving stiff limbs and rigid taut bodies, and some graceful and flowing involving swirling and turning arms, legs, hands, feet and bodies.

Activity 2: Kinds of movement in art

The distinctions made in kinds of movement done in PE in Activity 1 can be illustrated through art. Here are some examples:

● *Translation.* Straight strokes with a brush, using large sheets of paper. This makes excellent wrapping, book covers, backdrops for collage or abstract work.
● *Rotation.* Curling and turning, spirals in paint and print, taking your brush in any path across the paper, turning and printing, angles in prints.

Activity 3: Moving a programmable toy

Let the children program a toy to complete straight and turning movements.

Straight movements made these patterns

Curling and turning movements made these patterns

ANGLE, INCLUDING RIGHT ANGLES

Commentary

It is important to see different angles as being the result of a movement – a rotation. Rather than visualising an angle as some sort of measure between two lines joined at one end it is useful to imagine that one line is moving, rather like a hand on a clock. Indeed, the movements of the hands of a clock are useful in considering the idea of angle with children. Seeing angles as connected with rotation will help with the idea of a complete (360°) turn and, at a later stage, the possibility of greater than one turn.

Activity 1: Concept of angle

In a PE lesson ask the children to move about, changing direction abruptly at the sound of a clap or tambour. When they have done this a few times point out to them that the abrupt change of direction is tracing an 'angle' on the floor. Next ask them to make angular shapes with their bodies. They can do this by themselves and then in pairs.

Activity 2: Angles around us

Ask the children to look for angles in the environment. If they have already looked for right angles this will be an extra challenge, for they can search out angles other than right angles.

Copymaster 82 (Angles around school) gives the children an opportunity to list kinds of angles they find.

Activity 3: Angle in design

Create a display to include an Anglepoise® lamp, angle iron, information about the angled deck on aircraft, and a book on astronomy explaining the use of angular distance. Add to this models of three-dimensional shapes the children have made.

Activity 4: Following angle instructions

Now that the children have learned about themselves and angle, and have experimented at making angles with their bodies in Activity 1, they should be ready to follow instructions about angle. In a series of PE floor-work lessons, try getting them to turn through right angles and acute angles to create a short movement sequence. This can be shown in an assembly, or they can translate the movements into design, using chalks, paints or collage.

Activity 5: Angles and LOGO

Let the children use a LOGO software package on the school computer to move the 'turtle' through different amounts of a rotation (size of angle) and create patterns and shapes. (See also AT 3, Level 3, LOGO.)

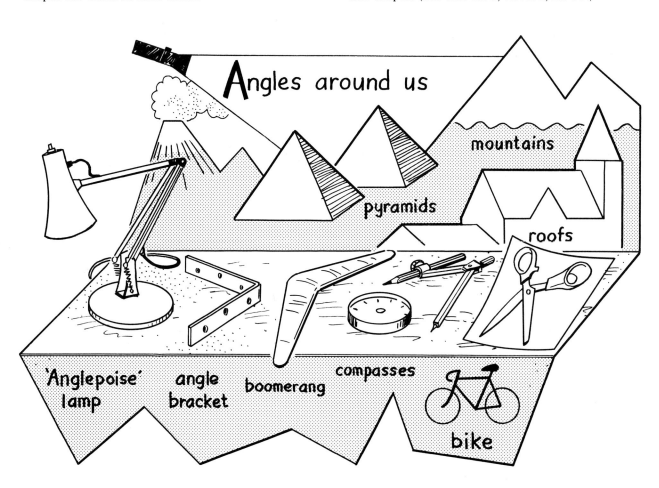

Angles around us

mountains

pyramids

roofs

'Anglepoise' lamp   angle bracket   boomerang   compasses   bike

FUN WITH SHAPE AND ANGLE

C83

Commentary

If you are to keep children free of the prejudice that mathematics is sums, or at best squares and circles, and keep the joy in their learning, then enabling them to have fun with shape and angle is a chance to be really creative. The following widely diverse activities will all contribute to children's confidence with shape and pattern.

Activity 1: Silly walks

(With apologies to Monty Python!) Invite the children to invent as many ways as they can of getting about. You can talk about straight and turning movements, but the important thing is that the children have a chance to experiment and recognise the possibilities in moving themselves. This understanding will feed their understanding of shape and space in mathematics.

Activity 2: Play acting moving shapes
Create a series of shape characters and invent a one-act play. The events do not need to be fantastical: 'A meal out for Ann Square' or 'The Cuboids visit the library' would provide many opportunities for shape talk and meetings.

Copymaster 83 (Shape characters and play titles) presents the children with a selection of possible characters and titles from which they may choose, and to which they may add to invent a play. These could be acted out with children dressed as the characters. Make a video of it if you can.

Activity 3: Cartoons
Let the children invent some cartoon characters and tell of their adventures. They can say the story aloud while holding up a series of pictures, or create a picture that tells a story. Examples could include a story from the planet 'Angle' or 'The 2-D cat'.

CONSERVATION OF MEASURES

Commentary
Position and orientation are vital to the ability to conserve measures. Link measuring activities the children do to their work in PE, dance and shape, in order that study in one area will support understanding in others.

Conservation of a wide variety of measures in a range of situations is only achievable through practical experience. If, for example, you have tried cooking in someone else's kitchen, only to find that the pots seem to be all the wrong shapes and sizes, you will know that adults cannot conserve capacity in unfamiliar settings! The children's confidence in conserving measures will be directly related, therefore, to the breadth of the range of different measuring situations they have worked in.

Activity: Conservation discussion and demonstration
In discussion, present the children with a series of situations in which the conservation of measurement is clear. Here are a few starter examples:

● A teacher's table is the same length on every day of the week!
● We cannot lengthen a curtain by taking some off the top and adding it to the bottom.
● One bottle full of milk will make two, three or even ten drinks but there is still no more than a bottle full.
● An unopened bag of flour weighs the same on any scales, at any time (provided the scales are accurate!).

You can demonstrate conservation, but remember that evidence that the children can conserve in one situation is not necessarily generalisable to others.

REVIEW: SHAPE AND SPACE SO FAR

The children should now be 'into' shape, using mathematical jargon to describe their work with both two- and three-dimensional shapes and keen to try complex model-making. Work at this level has introduced them to angles, especially right angles, and to angle and movement. Check the following:

● Do they know the important characteristics of common two- and three-dimensional shapes?

● Do they recognise right angles?

● Do they know about types of movement?

Again it is important to take sufficient time over these basics and to give plenty of practical applications.

The children should also have been exposed to experiences that help them start to use standard measures and begin to conserve measurement.

Attainment Target 4: Shape and space, Level 3

Pupils should recognise and use the properties of two-dimensional (2-D) and three-dimensional (3-D) shapes and use measurement, location and transformation in the study of space.

Programme of study	Statements of attainment	Examples
Pupils should engage in activities which involve:	Pupils should be able to:	Pupils could:
• sorting 2-D and 3-D shapes and giving reasons for each method of sorting.	a) Sort shapes using mathematical criteria and give reasons.	*Sort shapes with a square corner, shapes with curved edges and shapes with equal sides or faces, giving appropriate explanations.*
• recognising (reflective) symmetry in a variety of shapes in two and three dimensions.	b) Recognise reflective symmetry.	*Explore patterns from a variety of world cultures, e.g. Islamic, Japanese.* *Study shapes and identify some lines and planes of symmetry.* *Explore patterns in art or PE.*
• using and understanding compass bearings and the terms 'clockwise' and 'anticlockwise'.	c) Use the eight points of the compass to show direction.	*Describe wind direction from a weather vane.* *Describe locations of places in the neighbourhood of the school, using compass points.*

SORTING 2-D SHAPES

C84
R4–7

Commentary
In many respects this work maps closely on to the work in Level 2. It is very much a consolidation of those earlier activities and provides you with an opportunity to remediate and/or extend the appreciation of two-dimensional shapes.

Activity 1: Sorting out
Using a selection of card and plastic two-dimensional shapes, sort them into sets. Ask the children to guess how they have been sorted. Let the children take it in turns to do the sort.

Arrange a display of the shapes when not in use so that the children can freely examine and sort them.

Activity 2: Attributes shapes
Buy or borrow a set of shapes, or better still, several sets of shapes that are mathematically accurate. Do 'sorts' with these. It will depend on what the set contains what 'sorts' are possible. Make sure that the children can recognise and identify right angles (Level 2), sides of equal length and numbers of corners or vertices.

Activity 3: Attributes quiz
Set the children a quiz which involves identifying shapes according to their attributes. For example, you could ask: 'Name two shapes which have four corners.' 'What is a shape with six sides called?'

There is a two-dimensional shapes quiz on **copymaster 84**.

Can you sort these shapes into sets?

Ask a friend to guess <u>how</u> you sorted them

Activity 4: LOGO
Set up the computer with LOGO software, and invite the children to produce shapes that are mathematically correct. The results can be printed out alongside the program invented, and this can be tried out by other children. Depending on their experience with computers and with LOGO (see Level 2), the children may need some help from you to make a start. This activity also helps to refine logical thinking.

Activity 5: Shape and pattern investigation
Make a collection of books about ancient civilisations, other cultures and pattern in art, and invite the children to choose a pattern and investigate its origins, or a civilisation or culture and investigate the patterns used. If the children are not ready for research in this way, choose, for example, 'The ancient Egyptians', 'Patterns from the East', or 'North American Indians' and find out some of the main pattern forms in use. With the stimulus of books, pictures, fabrics and maybe even objects with patterns on them, the children will be able to explore and replicate the shapes used in pattern-making. The outcome would make a stunning display.

You may find the children enjoy producing patterns on squared paper (**resource copymasters R4** and **R5**) or on 'dotty' paper (**resource copymasters R6** and **R7**).

SORTING 3-D SHAPES

Commentary
Again we are looking at the consolidation of earlier work. The children should now be coming to a skilled recognition of similarities and differences between three-dimensional shapes. They should be recognising and naming shapes and be able to pick out shapes in the environment.

Activity 1: Sorting out
Use a collection of cartons, boxes and containers to make shape sets. Let the children identify the basis for the sort, and then do 'sorts' for themselves.

Activity 2: Attributes blocks
Using a set of shapes that are mathematically accurate, like Logiblocks® (which offer not only shape, but size,

colour and thickness) or Poleidoblocs® (which include cones and pyramids), let the children do the sorting using one or more criteria (see AT 5: Handling data, Level 2). They can record some of the outcomes of the sorts using Venn or Carroll diagrams, for example.

Resource copymasters R8–10 (Venn diagrams) and **R11** (Carroll diagram) will help children with their recording of sorts.

Activity 3: Attributes quiz
Give the children a quiz involving the attributes of three-dimensional shapes. You could ask, for example: 'Which shape has two triangular faces?' and 'Which shapes have eight corners?'
Copymaster 85 is a three-dimensional shapes quiz.

Activity 4: Shape in buildings
Look at the school buildings and those in neighbouring streets and determine the shapes in common use. Discuss with the children why these shapes are used. Ask the children to draw buildings using shapes different from those they have seen, and to comment on the advantages and disadvantages of the new shapes.

Activity 5: The shape of our school
Make a model of the school. It need not be accurately to scale for the children may find accurate measurement difficult at this stage, but the shape must reflect the actual look of the school. Display the model with a discussion of the process of modelling and the kinds of shapes that had to be considered and incorporated.

New shapes for school buildings!

Jack's model school

Megan drew tall towers

Olive put the playground in the middle of the school.

Joseph's school has more space for flowers

Activity 6: The built environment
Look at buildings around the school, particularly those with a variety of shapes in them. You may, for example, be near the village church or the market cross, the Corn Exchange, mill or Town Hall. The children may want to investigate shapes in popular use a long time ago.

Activity 7: Model-making
When setting children model-making tasks, you can use shape names and attributes, and expect quite sophisticated outcomes. You can tie this work in with their technology activities. Here are some examples of the kinds of tasks to set:

- Archways and tunnels
- Towers
- Structures that lean
- Structures that have a small base and large top.

In all cases the children can display and discuss their efforts.

Activity 8: Shape in everyday expressions
With the children's help, collect together sayings and expressions which use shape and space in the wording. Discuss what we mean when we use these. Examples include:

- 'It is as broad as it is long'
- 'Get to the point'
- 'Rounding off'
- 'Keep to the straight and narrow'
- 'There is no side to her'
- 'Being on edge'.

SYMMETRY

Commentary

The two forms of symmetry that children will identify given the opportunity are line or reflective symmetry and rotational symmetry. Of these it is expected that reflective symmetry will be commonly recognised by children at this Level.

Reflective symmetry means that a line drawn through a shape will give two halves of the shape which are mirror images of each other. An example would be a line through the centre of the unequal side of an isoceles triangle and the opposite angle. An equilateral triangle has three lines of symmetry. A circle has an infinite number.

Rotational symmetry means that a shape can be rotated and at certain positions will look like the shape at its starting point. Examples are the letter S and a child's windmill.

Activity 1: Ink-blots and butterflies

Cut paper to various shapes and sizes. Make sure the paper is partially absorbent, that is, neither too glossy nor too absorbent, or it will make this task difficult for the children to do without making a mess. Fold each piece along the centre line. Let the children put blobs of paint or water-based ink on the paper, and then fold it along the crease and rub gently to spread the paint or ink a little. When they open up the paper the resulting picture has two matching halves (one axis of symmetry). This work can be used for book covers, mobiles and display.

Patterns with one axis of symmetry

Activity 2: Cutting folded paper

Cut paper to various shapes and sizes. Fold the paper along a centre line. Ask the children to cut out a shape, through both thicknesses, starting by cutting across the fold. When the paper is opened out the children will see that the fold marks the axis of symmetry of the picture.

Activity 3: 2-D shapes with one axis of symmetry

Supply the children with a box of two-dimensional shapes and some plane 'plastic' mirrors. Let them explore with shapes they can put the mirror on, and re-create the shape perfectly.

Copymaster 86 (2-D shapes and symmetry) offers children a range of shapes and they can decide which are symmetrical (some have more than one axis of symmetry).

Activity 4: Folding shapes

Give the children some scraps of paper which are irregular shapes, and some regular shaped pieces. Ask them to try folding the pieces of paper, to see which offer symmetrical halves and which do not.

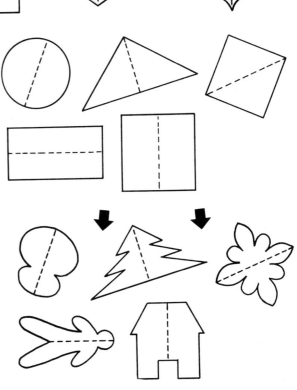

93

Activity 5: Symmetry, pairs and left and right

Show the children that one axis of symmetry offers two halves which match, and that this match marks a left and a right as in feet, shoes, hands, mittens and eyes! Practise left and right and give the children the chance to match their own lefts and rights on a display.

On the classroom door, on the side where the door opens away (so that the children do not get hit on the nose!) stick down two giant footprints on the floor. Mark these left and right. On the door attach two giant hands and mark them left and right. Cover them with clear film for they will get a lot of use. The children can stand on the giant footprints and match their hands to the handprints.

Activity 6: 2-D shapes with more than one axis of symmetry

Check out all the shapes in your classroom collection with the children to see which have more than one axis of symmetry. Create a symmetry classbook that offers puzzles and shape facts to the children.

Activity 7: Symmetry in numerals

Let the children draw and colour the numerals 1 to 10, or their age numeral, or the number of their house, and then work out and draw in the axes of symmetry in these, if any.

Copymaster 87 (House number symmetry) is a sheet on which to record their own or their friend's house number, and then look at what they can do to it with a plane mirror.

Activity 8: Symmetry in letters

Let the children draw and embellish their own name in capital letters. They can then see which letters have axes of symmetry and where the axes lie.

Copymaster 88 (Letter symmetry) gives the children the chance to play with axes of symmetry in letters of their own name using a plane mirror.

Activity 9: 3-D shapes and planes of symmetry

Try cutting a matchbox, a cuboid of cheese, an apple or orange and a (firm!) marshmallow across some of their planes of symmetry and showing them to the children. If you can get hold of matching food boxes, you can lay them together, pretend they are one box, and then show a plane of symmetry where they part.

Planes of symmetry are quite difficult to demonstrate in a drawing. With your help, and using straws or card strips, the children could make skeleton models of, for example, a cuboid, a cube, a prism and a pyramid. Using pieces of thin paper, you can demonstrate where the planes of symmetry lie.

Another possibility is for you yourself to cut Plasticine® shapes through the planes of symmetry.

Copymaster 89 (Planes of symmetry) gives children the chance to enter how many planes of symmetry are found in some shapes.

DIRECTION ON COMPASS AND CLOCK

Commentary

There are two mathematical opportunities offered by the use of the magnetic compass. They are to develop the notion of rotations and angles, and to lay some of the foundation for later work on maps and co-ordinates.

The most common device that embodies a rotational turning motion is the 12-hour clock. Like the use of left and right the terms 'clockwise' and 'anti-clockwise' are centrally important concepts in society.

Activity 1: Which is north?

Show the children a pocket compass. Set it down on the table, explaining that it must be kept *away* from computers, videos and watches for it may upset the workings of these machines. Swivel the compass until the magnet's 'N' lines up with N on the dial. Point in that direction and tell the children that that is north. Place a large cardboard arrow on the table so that it points north.

Stick a sign on the floor in the classroom, which points north.

Take the children into the playground. Orientate the compass again and draw a chalk mark on the playground to show north.

95

Activity 2: Four main directions

Show the children a weather vane or pictures of one and some designs of the points of the compass, like those that appear on old maps. Let the children make their own. If they line up their drawing so that their north matches the direction of the north stuck on the floor in Activity 1, they will be able to say which is south, east and west.

There is the basis for a compass drawing that the children can embellish on **copymaster 90** (Points of the compass).

Activity 3: Where are we?

Look at some large-scale maps of your locality, Ordnance Survey maps and maps of the British Isles. Look for the compass sign, and investigate which towns and cities, mountains and rivers, lakes and coastlines are to the north, south, east and west of the school.

Activity 4: Where on Earth? A look at a globe

Take a close look at a globe. Get the children looking for the north pole, the south pole, the United Kingdom and for which nations are to the north, south, east and west of the United Kingdom.

Activity 5: All eight compass points

Look again at the designs and homemade compass patterns from Activity 2 and introduce all eight points on the compass. The children can draw another compass pattern, putting in all eight points.

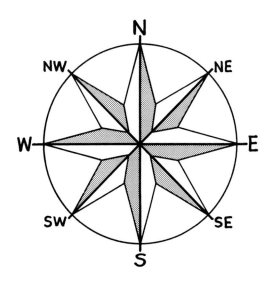

Activity 6: Finding your way

Make up a trail the children can try in pairs around the school. They can take a compass and follow the directions. For example:

Take six paces north.
Go through the doorway.
Walk east until you reach a big step.
Step down.
Take four strides west ...

and so on. The children can then make up a trail for themselves, which they can put to the test.

Copymaster 91 (Compass trail) is for children to record their trail. These trails could go into a book from which they could choose one to try when they have a few minutes at the end of a task.

Activity 7: Clockwise and anti-clockwise

Using a large cardboard clock face, show the children the direction in which the clock goes, and tell them that it is called clockwise. Play at turning round clockwise and drawing a circle clockwise. Let one child walk around a circle of children in a clockwise fashion.

In a separate session introduce the concept of anti-clockwise, using similar examples to those given above.

Copymaster 92 (Clockwise and anti-clockwise) gives the children the opportunity to interpret clockwise and anti-clockwise arrows on illustrations.

Activity 8: Direction of turn

Let the children examine and use screws and screwdrivers, screw-top jars, keys in locks, keys on clockwork toys, and knobs on baby toys to find out whether they go clockwise or anti-clockwise. Label them and mount a display.

Find out and say which way they turn.

REVIEW: SHAPE AND SPACE SO FAR

Throughout this section we have stressed the need to relate the perception of different sorts of shapes, and the spaces between them, to both natural and designed environments. The study of shape and space has never been a purely abstract area of study; it has always had its roots in physical representation and application. When the ancient Greeks formulated geometrical theorems, their starting point was observation of real shapes and relationships. It is vital that we offer children practical activities for them to consolidate and expand their spatial awareness and their spatial concepts. Activities in the built environment can help a lot with this.

This is the Level at which the children should have consolidated all their work on common two- and three-dimensional shapes, and should also now have an understanding of the points of the compass and clockwise and anti-clockwise rotation.

97

ATTAINMENT TARGET 5
Handling data

Attainment Target 5: Handling data

Pupils should collect, process and interpret data and should understand, estimate and use probabilities.

It is on the basis of data that we manage our lives. Much of our decision-making is based upon the assembling of data, its interpretation and the prediction of likely events based upon that interpretation. The exent to which we make decisions that are reasoned and reasonable has much to do with the quality, scope and analysis of data. On the other hand, we can leave it all to fate! From these statements you will gather that we see data handling as being an important area of application in mathematics.

Many people hold a range of superstitions which sometimes affects their decision-making. We all know about lucky heather, not walking under ladders, Friday the 13th and what happens if we spill the salt! It is interesting how powerful, at times, is the sense that the coin will come down heads or that the fruit machine will pay out the jackpot at the next spin of the reels. But if we examine probabilities using mathematical techniques our sense of luck is questionable. While it is nice to dream and none of us would want to deprive children of their ability to immerse themselves in myths and legends and exciting stories, it is equally important that we give them the tools that will enable them to distinguish between sensible choices and sheer fantasy. In the past we have not done very much on the probability and chance aspects of data handling in the primary sector. The National Curriculum has changed that.

Besides examining the basis of much of our data collection in terms of its validity another important facet is the discipline of data collection. As in science there is a need to organise the format and scope of any data collection activity and then have the persistence to carry through that data collection – and to do so without starting to interpret what is being collected too soon. Leaping to conclusions on the basis of partial data is not acceptable and this is one of the often difficult things that we need to draw out of our data handling work. Additionally, of course, it is important to help the children to see that different sources of data may need tapping in different ways and this is also part of a planned data collection activity. The form in which data comes will affect the ways in which it can be analysed and interpreted.

Presenting data in an understandable and clear form is the final piece of the jigsaw, since constructing meaningful pictorial representations needs the author of the work to have understood that data. It is also the case that the choice of representation must be sensibly linked to the type of data and its organisation.

So data handling is a complex activity characterised by the need to plan, the need to be patient and persistent, and the need to have a wide repertoire of techniques and methods of presentation at your fingertips. The early work in data handling sets out to establish important foundations in all of these areas.

Resourcing this section

You need data! You can get it at second hand, by looking for lists, tables, frequency charts and block graphs already available. Though these are important they do not replace the first-hand data that the children as researchers collect in school. It may also be useful to have a cardboard grid similar to dividers in wine boxes to start the children off in making concrete block graphs.

Attainment Target 5: Handling data, Level 1

Pupils should collect, process and interpret data and should understand, estimate and use probabilities.

Programme of study	Statements of attainment	Examples
Pupils should engage in activities which involve:	Pupils should be able to:	Pupils could:
• selecting criteria for sorting a set of objects and applying them consistently.	a) Sort a set of objects, describing the criteria chosen.	Sort a collection of objects of various shapes, sizes and properties.
• recording with objects or drawing and commenting on the results.		E.g.: Sort items of shopping by placing them next to the symbol for dinner 🍽 or pudding 🥘
• creating simple mapping diagrams showing relationships and interpreting them.		
• recognising possible outcomes of random events.		

SORTING ▶

Commentary

Many children will be familiar with sorting before they come to school. If parents have let them sort the washing into whites and coloureds, the shoes into pairs or the shopping from the basket, they will be able to put things together, and say what is the same about them.

The focus in the activities below is on developing the children's strategies for choosing criteria for sorting.

Begin with a single criterion for sorting – for example, aged 6/not aged 6 – and later introduce two or three sorts which may overlap.

Activity 1: Beginning sorting

If the children have already done work in other sections of this book, they will have had practice in sorting in school. If you are starting them here, begin with the children themselves. Sort a group out according to whether, for example, they are boys or girls, they have blonde hair or not, they have long or short socks. At first you may need to tell the children how you have made the sort. Soon they will be able to guess.

Let them take turns at sorting out the rest of the group while the group members guess the basis of the sort.

Activity 2: Sorting children's belongings

Having used the children themselves in Activity 1 you can now turn to the next resource to the children themselves, namely their possessions. Play at sorting hats and coats, shoe bags and pencil cases, plimsolls and lunch boxes.

Let the children do some sorting of these and guess the criteria for each other's sorts.

Activity 3: Sorts using pictures

Let the children use a selection of toys and equipment from the classroom or pictures from magazines. If the pictures are mounted on card and laminated they will remain usable for several groups of children. As with the sorts in Activities 1 and 2, begin by doing some yourself and letting the children guess the basis of the sort. Then let them sort for each other. When not in use these things can be laid out on a table, so that the children can handle and sort them themselves.

Our Sorting table

STORIES

Sort the toys into sets

99

Activity 4: About children
Use information about the children to put them into sets. Here are some suggestions:

- Those who have/have not a pet cat
- Those who have/have not a brother
- Those who live/do not live in a flat
- Those whose house has/has not a back garden.

You can also make two- or three-way sorts, depending on the size of the group of children. For example:

- Live in a flat/bungalow/house
- Have/have not a brother/have more than one brother.

This information makes excellent material for you to put in a class book which can be added to the maths resources. Though the children should not be made to record their sorts you could use pictures of 'Heather's cat' and 'Kelvin's house' to illustrate the book.

Activity 5: How many ways can you sort?
Show the children a small number of items for sorting, about six in all. The challenge is, without moving them at all, they should think of as many ways of sorting them as possible. You can then ask a child to show all the sorts, and then add the other children's new ideas. This activity will give you a way of assessing whether the children have mastered the concept of sorting.

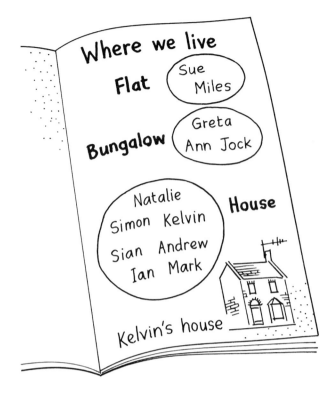

FIRST RECORDING

Commentary
Several times in this book we have asked that the children should not be expected to record too soon. When handling data, in order to collect and organise it, the children will need to record, if only to support their memories. They should still have plenty of sorting without recording before committing anything to paper.

Activity 1: Concrete records
Let the children assemble and order data about themselves and things around them by physically using the children and the equipment. For example, if a child has made a sort of his/her work group into those wearing/not wearing red, he/she can physically line up the 'red wearers' apart from the 'not red wearers'. The range of data available about the children and equipment in the room is remarkably wide, but here are some possible starter suggestions:

- *The children themselves*
  - Aspects of clothing
  - Hairstyles and length
  - Eye colour
  - Foot or shoe size.

- *The children's belongings*
  - Colours/sizes of shoe bag
  - Styles of schoolbag
  - Size of plimsolls
  - Break-time snacks (using the wrappers as the data).
- *Classroom equipment*
  - Sets of shapes
  - Pencils according to size/colour
  - Soft toys
  - Crayons or chalks.

Activity 2: Freehand drawing
The first step in recording data on paper is by drawing. At first let the children record on plain paper, without attempting to organise their recording for them. The sources of data are numerous, and you can also use pictures the children have drawn in other contexts. If, for example, Anthea has drawn herself and her dog, this is a recording of data about herself and demonstrates one-to-one correspondence. When Fred draws the class goldfish, he may not only record the set of goldfish, but also the number of goldfish and some data about their habitat. Of course the drawings children do in relation to sets in maths are relevant here.

Activity 3: Colouring in

When the children have drawn information about the data they are working with, you may like to introduce colouring as a recording activity. If you supply a picture of a train and ask Mandy to colour the first carriage blue, by colouring appropriately she is recording data. In a picture with several shapes, you can ask Hussein to colour just the triangles. Hussein then represents the number of and characteristics of triangles by 'tagging' them with a colour. Many commercially produced maths schemes rely on this kind of recording.

Activity 4: Using templates

Let children use templates to record information. Giving children templates can help to reduce the number of skills they bring to bear on a task, and make the outcome more to their satisfaction. These can include shapes to draw round, shapes to stick on and shapes to print. For example:

● Melanie can draw round a rectangle to represent the number of windows in the classroom
● Mick can stick on circles to show the ladybirds on the school rose bush
● Tina can print a potato cut for every girl in the class.

Hussein coloured the triangles

Mandy coloured the first truck blue

These colourings give us information. Can you find the **triangles**... ...and the **first truck**?

Melanie

Windows in the classroom

Ladybirds on a bush   Mick

Girls in our class   Tina

MAPPING

C93, 94

Commentary

The idea of correspondence and, in particular, one-to-one correspondence (whether of one thing or one group of things) is an important concept. 'Mapping' like this lies at the root of being able to build the notion of functions in mathematics and the portrayal of relationships through graphical representation.

Activity 1: Concrete one-to-one correspondence

Let the children use each other as their first resource. They can, for example:

● match boy to girl to make 'pairs'
● match shoe bag or coat to child
● match lunch box or snack to child

101

If you have a play house the children can also use the toys from that to demonstrate one-to-one correspondence. For example:

● Bowls, chairs and beds for teddies
● Pram, cover, rattle for dolly.

Activity 2: Mapping one-to-one
When the children are ready to record their concrete mapping activities, you can let them draw, for example, the three bears, each with a bowl, or themselves with their pet or a pencil or book each. You can then give the children mapping exercises to do, using pictures.

There are some starter ideas on **copymaster 93** (Mapping).

Activity 3: Talk about mapping
The idea behind one-to-one correspondence is familiar to children in everyday life. However, they need not only to be able to do it, but also to be able to talk about what they are doing. Let the children tell each other of their mapping activities as they do them, and present what they have done with an oral explanation.

Activity 4: Complex mapping
One-to-one correspondence is the most familiar form of mapping. When the children are confident about doing this and articulate in talking about it, they will be able to handle more complex mapping. Try some of these examples:

Big Ted   Midi Ted   Baby Ted

Big Ted's bowl   Midi Ted's bowl   Baby Ted's bowl

● Teacher to children (one-to-many)
● Families – children to parents or kittens to cats (many-to-many)
● Coloured pencils to child (many-to-one).

There are some examples on **copymaster 94** (Complex mapping).

102

BEGINNING PROBABILITY

Commentary

Assessing probabilities seems to be fundamental to human survival! You need to know what the chances are that a car will hit you, a dog will bite, or a hot drink scald your tongue before you take a risk. In all these examples you do need prior knowledge, if not experience, to make realistic judgements. It is rather like estimation.

Many small children seem very adept at judging positive probabilities (as the look on the face of a two-year-old at the sight of a chocolate bar shows!). Parental protection prevents their contact with the negative kind. Probability is not about what is nice and what is nasty, good or bad, but simply the likelihood of something occurring.

You need to arm the children with sufficient facts and experience (which may be at second hand for not every child needs to be bitten by a dog before they know that dogs may bite) so that children can begin to assess probabilities of all kinds.

Activity 1: Possibilities in daily routine

Once children have had practice in going through the routine of a school day many times, they will be able to assess the probabilities that PE will be on Wednesday or that assembly will follow playtime. You can begin their experience of making these assessments by discussing with them the idea of 'probability' and 'chance'. There are also aspects of their daily routine at home which they can tell you about. Questions like, 'What do you do first when you get up?' or 'What does mum say as you leave the breakfast table?' may produce answers like, 'I always put my slippers on' or 'Most days mum reminds me to clean my teeth.' These are statements about probabilities.

Activity 2: Predicting outcomes

Show the children a coin and a die. Ask them what will be the outcome if you toss the coin or roll the die. Discuss their answers with them. They should be able to predict that the coin will show either a 'head' or 'tail', and that the die will show a number from one to six. Discuss with the children the possible outcome of a human pregnancy, litter size in cats and dogs, what kind of seed will grow on a plant, and similar events. Put the results of the discussions in a class book or on a chart.

Activity 3: Testing outcomes

You can let the children do some simple experiments to demonstrate outcomes. The problem is that in a small number of trials your results may not show the pattern predicted, so do bear this in mind. Let the children flip a coin a fixed number of times (say 20) and using rubber stamps bearing pictures of 'head' and 'tail' let them stamp them in two columns.

Put a number of blocks or beads of two colours into a bag (perhaps 4 red and 4 green). If the children take out a bead a fixed number of times (about 10) returning the bead to the bag after each 'go', they can record the colours obtained.

REVIEW: HANDLING DATA SO FAR

The way you choose to cover this section of mathematics will depend on your approach to mathematics teaching and the kind of planning and organisation you favour. Without dipping into this part of the book at all, you may feel the children are already able to do the following:

- Sort things out, and say how they have sorted them
- Record and map data
- Predict outcomes of events.

We felt it important to make handling data discrete because a quick review of the activities we have included will allow you to check coverage, and easily fill any gaps in the children's experience.

103

Attainment Target 5: Handling data, Level 2

Pupils should collect, process and interpret data and should understand, estimate and use probabilities.

Programme of study	Statements of attainment	Examples
Pupils should engage in activities which involve:	Pupils should be able to:	Pupils could:

Programme of study

Pupils should engage in activities which involve:

- choosing criteria to sort and classify objects; recording results or outcomes of events.
- designing a data collection sheet, collecting and recording data, leading to a frequency table.
- constructing and interpreting frequency tables and block graphs for discrete data.

Statements of attainment

Pupils should be able to:

a) Interpret relevant data which have been collected.

Examples

Pupils could:

Collect data on those children who walk to school and those who travel by bus or car. Illustrate with a block graph and draw simple conclusions.
Means of transport to school.
Pupils

Record the number of birds visiting the bird table and say which birds come most often:

Blackbird	XX	2
Sparrow	XXXXX	5
Robin	X	1
Blue Tit	XXX	3

Sort objects collected:

- using diagrams to represent the result of classification using two different criteria, e.g. Venn and tree diagrams.

- recognising that there is a degree of uncertainty about the outcomes of some events and that other events are either certain or impossible.

b) Recognise that there is a degree of uncertainty about the outcome of some events but that others are either certain or impossible.

Recognise that it is:

certain   *that 'someone somewhere will cough before the end of next week';*

impossible   *that 'Jane will be two metres tall by her eighth birthday';*

uncertain   *whether 'it will rain next week'.*

104

CHOOSE CRITERIA, SORT AND RECORD

R8
–11

Commentary

Following on from the opportunities that you will already have given to children to sort on limited criteria, provided by you, we are now at the stage where the children need to be able to start offering their own criteria.

As well as taking responsibility for sorting, the children should also be making decisions about how to record. Their repertoire of recording approaches can be extended.

Angelina did the sorting today. Can you work out how?

Ideas box

Paper and pencils

Activity 1: Guess my sort

If the children have had much practice at sorting at Level 1, they should now be able to carry through a sort of their own devising, from the initial stage of assembling the collection of objects or deciding the categories of data, through to recording the outcomes. As a preliminary to this process, let them take turns at doing sorts and see if their friends can guess the basis for the sort. They can do this in classtime, while you look on or visit the group every few minutes, or you can set up a sorting table and allow each child to assemble a number of sorts each day, leaving them on display. Others in their group can predict the bases for these sorts and put their ideas into a suggestion box. You can then gather the group together to discuss the sorts each day.

Activity 2: Recording results of sorts

The children can devise their own ways of recording the sorts that they do. When they have developed a range of ways, you can show them any which they may not have thought of, including, for example, the following:

● Venn, Carroll or tree diagrams (see page 108)
● String and collage
● Folding or partitioning paper
● Charts.

Resource copymasters R8 (Venn diagram: two discrete sets) and **R9** (Sets: four discrete) present blanks recording sorts of discrete sets. Use **resource copymasters R10** (Venn diagram: two overlapping sets) and **R11** (Carroll diagram) for more complex sorts.

FREQUENCY TABLES

C95
–7

Commentary

The kind of data you choose for frequency table work depends on the location of the school and classroom and the number of children in the group. If the data has to be collected spasmodically you want to avoid the children wasting time waiting, when nothing is happening; you also want a fair rate of data input to maintain the children's motivation. Thus, predicted occurrence should be your guide to deciding what information to collect.

We have included the design of data collection sheets as a separate activity, because the children need to have mastered all the necessary research skills to data collection and presentation in order to understand the problems in research design.

Activity 1: Putting information in order

Discuss with the children the reasons why we put information in order, on charts and so on. Show the children things which demonstrate information put in order. Make a display to which they can bring things to add. Here are some starter examples:

● Lists including
  – the register
  – a shopping list
  – a supermarket receipt
  – a library index
  – a book index.

● Tables including
  – the ingredients in foodstuffs (from packaging)
  – a train timetable
  – washing powder user instructions
  – postage required for weights of letters.

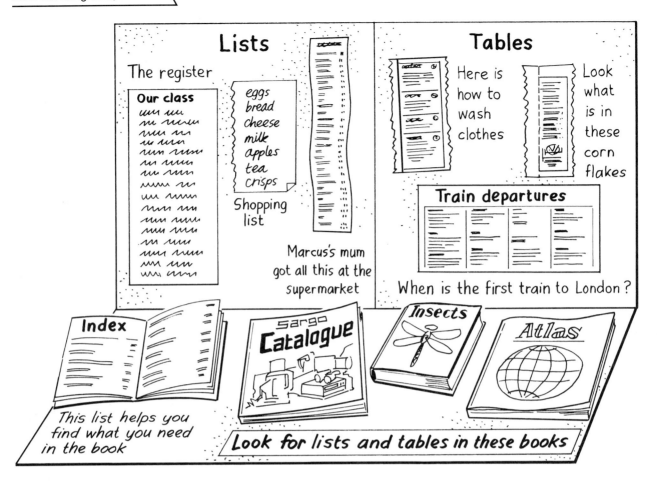

Note that the children do not need to fully understand how to interpret all these data sources at this Level – work at Level 3 supports this. You can also produce some data which has not been ordered and show the children how difficult it is to interpret.

Point out to the children that there are lots of ways of presenting information, and that we try to choose a way of setting it out that is easy to understand and gives ready access to the kind of information we will be needing. For example, if we repeatedly needed to work out which children lived closest to school, and then those that lived a little further away, and so on, teachers would keep a list of children, not alphabetical in terms of name, but perhaps by street name, starting with that closest to school.

Activity 2: How often?

The sources for the kind of information that children can easily transfer to a frequency table are legion. You could, for example, look at one of the following:

- Number of children in which class who pass your classroom door
- Number of aircraft flying over the school in the morning/afternoon
- Number of times a few common words like 'the', 'and' and 'is' appear in a short book
- Number of sunny days in a month.

Because the children cannot create a frequency table before they can interpret one, it may be a good idea to let them work on some ready-made data first.

Mrs Muddle's shopping list

Mrs Muddle's shopping
Can you see what she forgot to buy?

There are some imaginary data and a frequency chart on **copymaster 95** (Weather frequency table) which the children can discuss. **Copymaster 96** (Frequency data collection) is a suggested layout for the collection of data for a frequency chart. This could be added to a child's work file, when complete.

106

Activity 3: Designing data collection sheets

Suggest an experiment in data collection that the children may try. It may be one of those mentioned in Activity 2, or it may be, for example, the number of times the classroom door is opened in the first hour of schooling, every day for a week, or the number of times the school hamster uses its playwheel during each school day for a week. Ask the children what kinds of information they need to collect and for suggestions as to ways it could be laid out. If they suggest more than one way, they could share out the ways of collecting information and try them. The outcomes of the work can be displayed.

Activity 4: Interpreting frequency charts

The children will need an understanding of how to interpret frequency charts in order to create and design them. The data children have collected can be added to a class resource bank and then used again by subsequent sets of children. You may ask successive sets of children to collect the same kind of data, so that you have some longitudinal indication of, for example, the number of aircraft that fly overhead, disturbing lesson time, or the number of times each of a range of books are read. If you have computer software enabling the creation of a database, this is just the kind of information which will be of interest, not only to you and the current set of children you teach, but subsequent sets of children and others working in the school.

Copymaster 97 (Customer frequency table) presents some imaginary data on a frequency table of people visiting various shops in a precinct, which you can use to demonstrate how the data can be interpreted, or which the children can write about. This is only an example, and not intended to replace first-hand data that children collect themselves.

BLOCK GRAPHS

C98, 99
R4, 5

Commentary

The characteristics of block graphs are that:

- each column is discrete

- the blocks are all visually clear

- each column has its own label

- they allow a mix of numbers on one axis and labels on the other.

Activity 1: Concrete block graphs

Dividers from wine boxes, or pieces of card that have been interlocked can be very useful here, for these form a ready-made grid which will support things. Prop the grid against a backing sheet on which you have stuck or drawn numerals.

For small collections this structure can then be used to show how many toys of each kind are in a set, how many marbles of each colour in a bag, how many of each kind of shell, and so on.

backing paper or card   wine box divider

bears | house | dolls | cars

Activity 2: Representative block graphs

The next best thing to being able to put a real object into the block graph is a representation of it. For example, if the children draw themselves, these pictures can be stuck onto block graph charts. These charts may show: months of birthdays, colour of eyes or hair, shoe size, age.

You can choose a symbol to place on the block graph which is self-explanatory. Here are some examples:

● Pictures of fruit to show favourite fruit
● Decorated matchboxes with tiny dolls peeping out to show bedtimes
● A design in colour to show favourite colours.

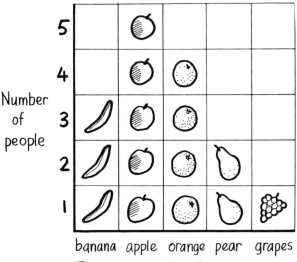

banana apple orange pear grapes

Favourite fruit

Activity 3: Using squared paper

Once the children have made concrete block graphs and representative block graphs they may find it straightforward to represent information on squared paper. You will need to mark in the axes for them, and work with them in counting the squares for each entry. They can then colour these in. You will know by your subsequent questioning whether they have a good understanding of what the squares of colour represent.

Resource copymasters **R4** and **R5** are for squared paper and **copymaster 98** is squared with axes drawn in. This may be appropriate for the block graphs the children do, depending on the numbers of items involved.

Activity 4: What goes on the axes?

For the children's first work on block graphs you will probably have decided on what goes along the axes and written it in. Try giving the children the opportunity of deciding how the information should be presented. If they come up with more than one suggestion, work through them with the children and see what the resulting graph looks like. The children should begin to make judgements about which presentation is clearer to them.

Activity 5: Assembling all the data

The next step is to let the children assemble the data they need for a block graph. Supply the children, working in pairs, with rough paper and a 'problem card'. It may say: 'Find out how many people's dads have moustaches, beards or are cleanshaven' or 'Test out which people in the class have ever eaten lychees, pomegranates, grapefruit and dates.' When they have collected the information ask them key questions like: 'How do you know you have asked everybody?' and 'How did you record people's answers?'

There are a number of problems set out on **copymaster 99**, which should be photocopied onto card, cut out and covered with protective film. These are examples of what the children may do, to which you can add suggestions related to the specific children with whom you are working.

Activity 6: Block graphs from start to finish

If the children have had practice in activities 1–5, they should now be able to have a go at collecting their own data and completing a block graph.

Remember there are axes drawn on squared paper on **copymaster 98**.

CARROLL, VENN AND TREE DIAGRAMS

Commentary

Classifying objects on the basis of two different criteria permits the use of a simple diagram for displaying the data. This offers opportunities for the future in that many simple classification keys are based on such distinctions, and the use of diagrams in mathematics is an important development of some mathematical ideas.

Activity 1: 'Concrete' Carroll diagram

Let the children sort a collection of objects, and then sort again within those sets. They will then have two

sets, each made up of two subsets. For example, if you give the children a collection of shapes, including triangles, squares and circles that are red, yellow or blue, they could sort them into circles/not circles and then red/not red.

If you then give the children a piece of paper which is divided into four quarters, they can place each subset of the shapes on one area of the paper. You can mark the sections 'circles'/'not circles' and 'red'/'not red'.

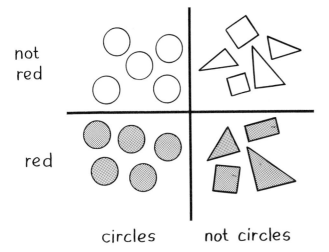

not
red

red

circles   not circles

Activity 2: Recording a Carroll diagram

Let the children try to do some sorts themselves and place them on a sectioned piece of paper like that used in Activity 1. On another piece of paper they can record what they have sorted and the criteria for the sort.

Resource copymaster R11 provides a grid suitable for Carroll diagrams.

Activity 3: 'Concrete' Venn diagram

Give the children a collection of objects which have been pre-selected by you to offer sorts according to two criteria. For example, you may give them red and blue beads that are spherical and cuboid.

Ask them to sort them out. They may choose red/not red. If they then sort by sphere/not sphere, they will have overlapping sets comprising 'red spheres', 'red not-spheres', 'not-red spheres', 'not-red not-spheres'. Let the children do a variety of sorts over a number of sessions.

Activity 4: Recording a Venn diagram

After plenty of practical sorts, the children can begin to record the results of their sorts on paper.

Resource copymasters R8 and **R9** are suitable for recording sorts of discrete sets, and **resource copymaster R10** for two overlapping sets.

Activity 5: Tree diagrams

Using real objects and drawing the results, let the children work on a sort to make a tree diagram. Here is an example using toy vehicles:

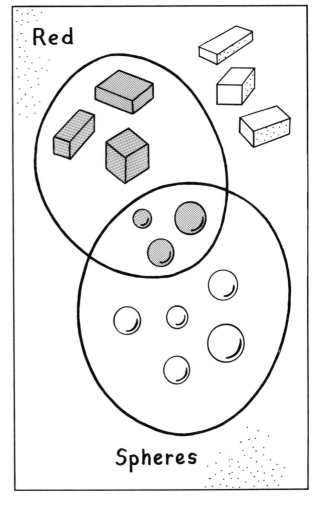

Red

Spheres

Activity 6: Making all the decisions

After practice the children should be able to select some things to sort, decide on the criteria for sorting, do the sort and present the outcomes in a Carroll, Venn or tree diagram. Their work can be displayed for other children to see.

Resource copymasters R8 to **R11** may help the children record their sorts in this activity.

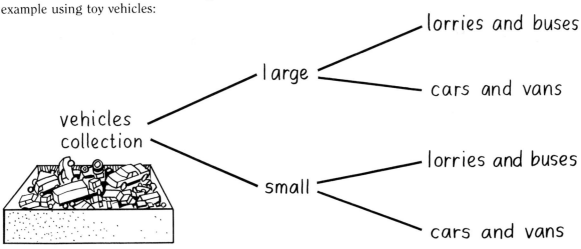

OUTCOMES OF EVENTS

Commentary

Some of the work expected here demands quite sophisticated thinking. There is much research to show that children (and even some adults) attribute to chance events aspects which logic tells us cannot be there. Placing a bet on a horse would not be an attractive option for some people if they did not believe that four times a winner means next time a winner, or that the outsider has a good chance of winning! However, research also shows that young children can be educated to assess degrees of uncertainty and chance. If you are prone to illogical estimations of chance yourself, keep your opinions from the young mathematicians in your care!

Activity 1: What is certain to happen?

This is a fascinating topic for discussion. It is (virtually) certain that:

● The world will not end tomorrow
● The sun will set tonight
● Night will fall
● Some children in your class will be 6 (or 7) next birthday.

See if the children can add to a list of happenings that are 'certain', which you can start a *Happenings* book with.

Activity 2: Degrees of uncertainty

Having established what can be said to be almost 'certain' the children can discuss what is 'uncertain' and why there is some doubt. This has to be handled sensitively, for children need to feel certain that mum will pick them up from school, and that there will be fish and chips for tea and so on. Try developing a path of happenings with 'Certain' ('Nightfall') at one end and 'Almost impossible' ('That mum will ask Clive to cook the tea tonight') at the other, with things like 'I will be able to stay up an extra half hour' or 'My picture will be in the paper tomorrow' somewhere in between.

Activity 3: Impossible happenings

Perhaps the children will regard it as impossible that they will ever be king or queen of England, that aliens will come to stay for the weekend, that human beings will all talk like Mickey Mouse tomorrow, or that cats all secretly speak Spanish. If you offer them a few equally ridiculous suggestions they will soon fill a book for the book corner, which they will pore over and relish.

REVIEW: HANDLING DATA SO FAR

Level 2 work has involved some considerable leaps for the children, particularly in relation to them operating independently and developing research management skills. The key is to take them through the processes many times, and on each occasion give them a little more control over the next step. In our experience children are eager to collect new information, less eager to organise it and tardy in collating and presenting it. However, if, with your guidance, they have persevered, they should now be able to do the following:

● Research where two variables are involved

● For a relatively small sample of respondents:
 – gather information
 – organise information in a block graph or Venn, Carroll or tree diagrams
 – interpret information presented in these ways.

The children should also be able to discuss the notion of predictability and consider the relative likelihood of named events.

Attainment Target 5: Handling data, Level 3

Pupils should collect, process and interpret data and should understand, estimate and use probabilities.

Programme of study	Statements of attainment	Examples
Pupils should engage in activities which involve:	Pupils should be able to:	Pupils could:
• extracting specific pieces of information from tables and lists. • entering and accessing information in a simple database, e.g. card database. • entering data into a simple computer database and using it to find answers to simple questions.	a) Access information in a simple database.	*Read off a value from a table; find the cost of an item in a mail order catalogue; compare the prices of similar items.* *Handle weather statistics or personal data, such as height, date of birth or age.* *Find information from simple bus or train timetables as part of planning a journey.*
• constructing and interpreting bar charts and graphs (pictograms) where the symbol represents a group of units.	b) Construct and interpret statistical diagrams.	*Decide what this graph tells you:* *Decide the number of raffle tickets sold by each class:*
• placing events in order of 'likelihood' and using appropriate words to identify the chance. • understanding and using the idea of 'evens' and saying whether events are more or less likely than this. • distinguishing between 'fair' and 'unfair'.	c) Use appropriate language to justify decisions when placing events in order of 'likelihood'.	*Explain why the following game is unfair:* *A bag contains 10 yellow and one red cube. The rules of the game are:* *– Player A is yellow; Player B is red;* *– the first player to pick his or her own colour out of the bag is the winner.* *Decide, for each of these statements, if they are 'very likely', 'likely', 'unlikely', or 'very unlikely':* *'Ten people in my class will be away tomorrow';* *'It will snow in the next half hour';* *'My favourite television star will visit my school';* *'We will do painting today'.*

INTERPRETING TABLES AND LISTS

Commentary
The children may have had the opportunity to begin this work at Level 2. It is a good opportunity to revise work for some children and for you to diagnose progress made so far.

Activity 1: Looking at lists
Use the assembly of lists that you had available at Level 2. If none have been collected or saved, start a collection, which may include the following:

● Shopping lists
● Supermarket receipts
● Lists of names, like the register, or the children who are doing cooking next
● A book with an index.

Inspect and discuss a selection of lists with the children. Locate items on the lists together and then see if the children can do this for themselves. Set the children some little problems that they can solve by looking at a list.

Copymaster 100 presents an imaginary shopping list with questions attached. There is also work on the index in a book, the title of which you or the child can write in.

Activity 2: Looking at tables
Collect tables which demonstrate a variety of data in a number of ways. You may include some of the following:

● A railway timetable
● Nutritional contents in foodstuffs
● Wash instructions on washing powder or liquid.

Look at some tables with the children and work out together how to access the information in them. At Level 2 there is a suggested display of lists and tables which could be replicated here, with more challenging questions for the children.

CARD DATABASES

Commentary
To show the children the principle of ordering information to allow easy entry, access and extraction, let them handle the permanent 'hard copy' of a card index.

Activity: Using a card index
Create and use a card index which is useful, not only as a resource for this activity, but also to your class or school. You may choose, for example, to catalogue the following on a card index:

● Maths resources throughout the school
● Location of charts and posters
● Location of 'special' resources
● Infant library books
● Children's information books
● Children's pets
● Children's sports and hobbies.

Show the children how the items are arranged, how to locate what they need and how to add new information.

WORK ON A COMPUTER DATABASE

Commentary
The introduction of computers into the classrooms and the growth in availability of user-friendly software in recent years makes the use of databases an integral part of all of our experiences. It takes the slog out of the organisation of data and allows all sorts of interrogations to take place.

Activity 1: Entering information
Using the software prompts and the results of discussion with the children, you need to set up the categories of information to be collected in the database. The children can then enter their own file of data onto the database. You can relate the database to a project you are doing, or with appropriate forward planning try

setting up two new databases each year. Soon the school will have a prodigious resource and files can be updated or added to year by year. Here are some starter ideas for databases:

- Ourselves: age, hair colour, eye colour, . . .
- Birds: size, habitat, colouring, wingspan, habits, diet, . . .
- Minibeasts: habitat, appearance, diet, . . .
- Weather: kinds, occurrence, effects on school-day, . . .
- Cooking/food: tried-and-tested recipes, nutrition needs of children, actual foods eaten, favourite foods, . . .

Activity 2: Accessing information
Using the software prompts let the children find things out using the database they have put on disc. For

example, if you have let them create a database about their families, they should then be able to retrieve information. You need to review what is in the database and then set questions. Here are some examples:

- How many children in the class have a grandad called William?
- How many children have two sisters?
- How many children are the 'only' child in a family?
- How many children live in a house with two bedrooms?

You will need to take care that the problems you set can be solved using the database. Some problems will need two or even three 'sorts' to list the required data.

BAR CHARTS

C98, 99

Commentary
Bar charts differ from block graphs in that the blocks are replaced by continuous bars. The lengths of the respective bars are the means by which the charts are interpreted.

Activity 1: What does a bar chart tell us?
Give the children a ready-made bar chart, for they need to be able to interpret one before they can construct

one. You could use a collection of play-dough animals or cakes to set beside a bar chart made about them. Then the children will be able to see the basis for the table. Let a number of children each choose their favourite from the array of animals or cakes. The bar chart may then look like this:

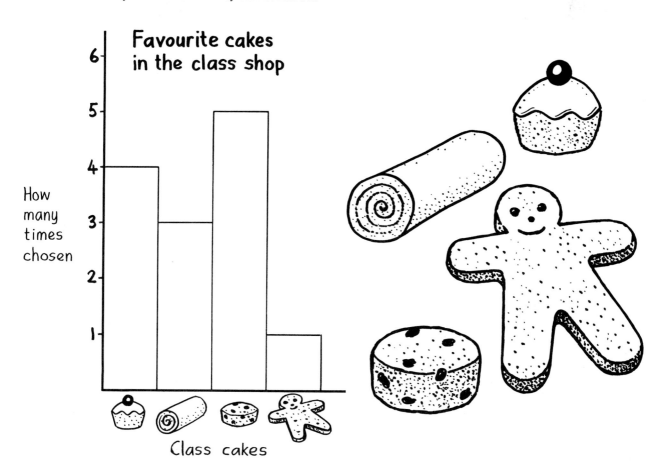

113

Activity 2: Constructing a bar chart

Now use another collection, similar to the one used in Activity 1, and let the children set out a bar chart. For example, you may use a selection of 'stock' from a class play shop. The resulting bar chart may look something like this:

Activity 3: Bar charts from beginning to end

Help the children decide on a category of data they may collect to put on a bar chart. Here are some starter suggestions:

● Favourite dinners
● Favourite colours
● What I want to be when I am grown up
● Hours of TV viewed in a week.

The children could work in twos, collect and collate the information (asking only a part of the class to keep the categories manageable), and compile a bar chart. These could be displayed or put into a class book.

There are axes drawn on squared paper ready for a bar chart on **copymaster 98**, and some sample problem cards on **copymaster 99**; these should be photocopied on to card, cut out and covered with adhesive film.

Play shop stock

SYMBOLIC PICTOGRAMS

Commentary
The children will already be good at interpreting symbols in all areas of their lives, including in mathematics. Now is a chance to tie this work in with safety symbols, danger symbols and symbols they use in mathematics.

Activity 1: Interpreting symbols
Give the children a variety of symbols to interpret. Arrange a display of symbols which they can inspect and interpret.

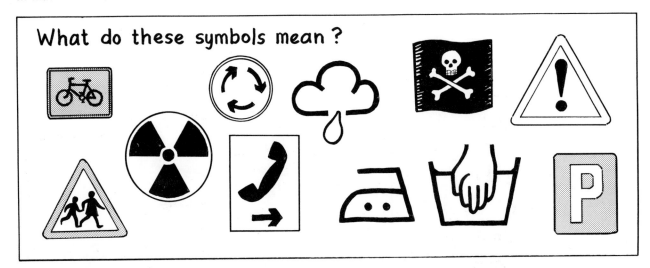

Activity 2: Interpreting pictograms
Show the children some ready-made pictograms with keys and help them to interpret the information.

Copymasters 101 and **102** are sample pictograms with keys. These are only examples and do not replace those you can compile using information of immediate importance to the children with whom you are working.

Activity 3: Creating symbols
Supply the children with some data which they can enter on a pictogram. For this activity they need to have the opportunity to create the symbol they will use. Here are some sample data worked through.

Data: **7** children clean their teeth once a day
15 children clean their teeth twice a day
4 children clean their teeth more than twice

Symbol: 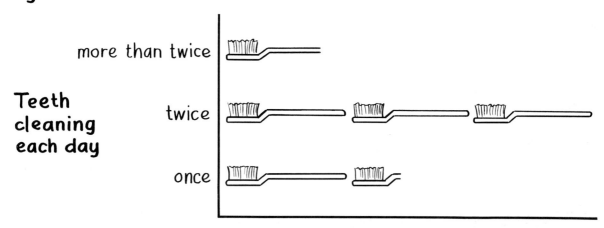 = 5 children

Pictogram:

more than twice

Teeth cleaning each day

twice

once

Activity 4: Creating pictograms
Let the children decide on the kind of data they can collect which will be suitable for a pictogram. Help them to compile a collecting sheet for the information.

The children could work in pairs for this task. When they have the information they can collate it, devise a symbol, or symbols for it and draw up the pictogram. Here is a compilation of the steps involved.

ESTIMATING CHANCES

Commentary

There are some quite sophisticated ideas embedded in this work and the children will have to have lots of opportunities to talk about the activities. You will also have to open up discussions about good luck and bad luck, for the children will already have their own ideas about these topics.

Activity 1: Using a chance 'scale'

Devise a chance 'scale' which illustrates the concepts you are trying to explain. You could, for example, use words like 'almost certainly will happen', 'very likely to happen', 'likely to happen', 'unlikely to happen', 'very unlikely to happen', 'almost impossible'. Compile a list of statements which the children can place in order of

the likelihood of their happening. You can include things like:

- I will wear shoes tomorrow
- There will be salmon sandwiches in my lunch box
- The weather tomorrow will be similar to the weather today
- My teacher is going to be a Hollywood film star when she retires.

Activity 2: Inventing a chance scale

When the children have worked on Activity 1 they will be able to write down their own scale of 'chance' and add items to it.

Copymaster 103 (Chance happenings) includes a list of items, some of which may serve to start the children off on their chance activities.

'EVENS' AND 'FAIR'

Commentary

Again there are quite sophisticated ideas underpinning the concepts of probability and the fairness of an event. You will need to give lots of different experiences to the children and their conclusions need to be talked through thoroughly.

Activity 1: What are 'evens'?

Collect a number of items which will show children the distinction between 'evens' and 'not evens'. Include the following:

- A coin
- Spinners with different numbers of sides (see **resource copymaster R1**)
- Dice with varying numbers of sides
- Playing cards
- Beads of different colours and cloth bags.

Show the children that, if there are only two possible outcomes, the chance of each is the same as the other each time, so we call this evens (provided it is fair). If there are more than two outcomes, the chance of each

particular outcome *is still the same each time* but is less than evens, and diminishes as the number of possibilities rises. Do remember that if you decide to put this to the test, a small number of trials may not produce a convincing result. If, for example, you toss the coin 20 times and it is 'heads' on 18 of those occasions, this does not actually support the 'evens' discussion! This does not shake the principle, however.

Activity 2: What makes a 'fair' test of chance?

Discuss this with the children. Chances are fair when not interfered with. The chance of getting 'heads' or 'tails' each time a coin is flipped is evens, unless the coin is bent, has two heads, is in the hands of someone who can flip it just enough for it to come down 'heads' each time, or there is some other reason for a change in the 'odds'.

When the children know this about a coin what can they say about a die, or spinner? The argument should be the same, despite there being a different chance of each number turning up.

REVIEW: HANDLING DATA SO FAR

In one sense the whole of living is about data handling. Even if we 'narrow' this down to what might be regarded as the mathematical aspects of data handling we are still faced with a considerable body of skills. With modern communications and a veritable explosion in the amount and diversity of information available to

us, data are collated and put before us continuously. Not a day goes by when we are not confronted by pie charts, block graphs, tables and so on in the newspapers. Even if we spurn news on the printed page we regularly see and hear the predictions of the weather forecasters! Having to try to cope with the interpretation of official forms, market research results, polls, pay rises, bills, holiday brochures and timetables is part of every adult's experience. We must therefore help children to acquire the skills to interpret, analyse, weigh up and respond to the data which will come their way. This is a demanding task, but one worth taking on. If the children can handle block graphs, databases, pictograms and know something about chance, you can feel they are not only skilled in handling the data that is the matter of all research, but they have established a level of mathematical understanding that is sadly beyond some adults.

RECORD SHEET

Name _____

AT	Level 1	Level 2	Level 3
1			
2			
3			
4			
5			